RESEARCH METHODS
TIPS AND TECHNIQUES

RESEARCH METHODS
TIPS AND TECHNIQUES

G. Vijayalakshmi

Reader
Department of Home Science
Gandhigram Rural University
Dindugal, Tamilnadu

C. Sivapragasam

Reader
Department of Applied Research
Gandhigram Rural University
Dindugal, Tamilnadu

MJP PUBLISHERS
Chennai 600 005

Impression: 2009

Cataloguing-in-Publication Data

Vijayalakshmi, G (1946 –).
Research Methods: Tips and Techniques / by
G. Vijayalakshmi, and C. Shivapragasam. –
Chennai : MJP Publishers, 2008
    xiv, 218 p. ; 21 cm.
    Includes References and Index.
    ISBN 978-81-8094-046-0 (pbk.)
    1. Research Methods I. Shivapragasam, C II. Title.
    001.42 VIJ MJP 039

ISBN 978-81-8094-046-0   **MJP PUBLISHERS**
© Publishers, 2008   47, Nallathambi Street
All rights reserved   Triplicane
Printed and bound in India   Chennai 600 005

Publisher : J.C. Pillai
Managing Editor : C. Sajeesh Kumar
Project Editor : P. Parvath Radha
Acquisitions Editor : C. Janarthanan
Assistant Editors : B. Ramalakshmi, S. Revathi
Composition : B. Ramalakshmi, N. Pushpa Bharathi,
L. Mohanapriya, N. Yamuna Devi,
Lissy John, M. Gnanasoundari
CIP Data : Prof. K. Hariharan

PREFACE

Research is a systematic search for more information and knowledge. In higher education, research is an academic programme and is considered as a prerequisite for awarding higher degrees. Progress in higher education is achieved by improving one's knowledge of the correct methodology of research. Research is part of all academic programmes at UG/PG/M.Phil./Ph.D. levels, both in arts and science. The students who are not familiar with the fundamentals of research waste a lot of time, energy and money in selecting the problem, in formulating the research design and writing the research report. Though there are several books and reference materials on research, user-friendly, first-level books/reference materials are still not nearer to the students for their use. Keeping in mind the needs of the students, we have attempted to provide in a simple manner details relating to planning and carrying out research studies, so that this book will serve as a good handbook for students taking up research work at all levels.

We owe a lot to Dr. S. Ponnuraj (husband of Dr. Vijayalakshmi) who has given us the inspiration and motivation and needed help to write this book. We would like to express our special thanks to our research students who, over the years, have done research under our guidance, as only their difficulties compelled us to write this book. We owe a great deal to the authors of those books we have referred to during the preparation of this book.

Our sincere thanks are due to Dr. S. Manivel who was kind enough to give valuable suggestions in completing this book.

We would like to express our thanks to Mr. A.M. Murugan who organised the typing and photocopying work, and Smt. A.P. Vedhavalli who typed the manuscript with skill and patience. We are also grateful to all our friends and colleagues who encouraged us to write this book. Our sincere thanks are also due to MJP Publishers, Chennai, for having come forward to publish this book.

Above all we are lgrateful to God for His blessings which have made the dream of writing this book a reality.

G. Vijayalakshmi
C. Shivapragasam

CONTENTS

1. FUNDAMENTALS OF RESEARCH 1

Meaning of Research 1

Purpose of Research 1

Characteristics of Research 2

Characteristics of a Researcher 2

2. CLASSIFICATION OF RESEARCH 5

Introduction 5

Pure Research 5

Applied Research 6

Exploratory Research 7

Descriptive Research 7

Diagnostic Study 8

Evaluation Study 9

Action Research 9

Experimental Research 9

Analytical Study or Statistical Method 10

Historical Research 10

Survey Research 11

Case Study 11

Field Studies 11

3. RESEARCH PROCESS   13

4. SELECTION ANALYSIS AND STATEMENT OF PROBLEM   15

    Introduction   15
    Problem Identification   15
    Prioritizing the Problem   17
        Relevance   17
        Avoidance of Duplication   18
        Feasibility   18
        Political Acceptability   18
        Applicability   18
        Urgency   19
        Ethical Acceptability   19
    Analysis of the Problem   21
    Statement of the Problem   22

5. REVIEW OF LITERATURE   25

    Need for Literature Review   25
    Sources of Information   25
    Steps Involved in Collection   26

6. FORMULATION OF RESEARCH OBJECTIVES   27

    General and Specific Objectives   27
        Need for Objectives   28
        Statement of Objectives   29
    Hypotheses   29
        Importance of Hypotheses   30
        Characteristics of a Good Hypothesis   31
        Types of Hypotheses   31

7. VARIABLES   33

    Introduction   33

    Variables—Meaning and Types   34

        Numerical Variables   34

        Categorical Variables   34

        Dependent and Independent Variables   34

        Active Variables   35

        Attribute Variables   35

        Composite Variables   35

        Confounding Variables   35

        Qualitative Variables   36

        Quantitative Variables   36

        Continuous Variables   37

        Universal Variables   37

    Selection and Statement of Variables   37

    Operationalizing Variables   38

8. TYPES OF STUDY   41

    Introduction   41

    Non-intervention Studies   42

        Exploratory Studies   42

        Descriptive Studies   42

        Analytical Studies   43

    Intervention Studies   48

        Experimental Studies   48

        Quasi-experimental Studies   50

        Before–After Study   51

9. DATA AND DATA COLLECTION TECHNIQUES
    AND TOOLS   53

    Introductions   53

    Classification of Data   53

       Primary Data   53

       Secondary Data   54

       Qualitative Data   56

       Quantitative Data   58

    Data Collection Techniques and Tools   **59**

    Using Available Information   59

       Observation   60

       Types of Observation, their Advantages
         and Disadvantages   60

       Tools for Observation   62

    Interviewing   64

       Purpose of Interviews   64

       Kinds of Interview   64

       Steps in Conducting an Interview   66

    Administering Written Data Collection Tools   68

       Questionnaires   68

       Attribute Scales   75

    Focus Group Discussion   79

    Importance of Combining Different
       Data Collection Techniques   79

    Characteristics of a Research Tool   80

       Reliability   80

       Validity   81

Practicability	83
Objectivity	84
10. SAMPLING	**85**
Introduction	85
Advantages of Sampling	85
Disadvantages of Sampling	86
Essentials of Sampling	87
Sampling Techniques	**87**
Probability Sampling	88
Simple Random Sampling	88
Stratified Sampling	90
Systematic Sampling	91
Multi-Stage Sampling	92
Cluster Sampling	93
Non-Probability Sampling	94
Judgement Sampling	94
Convenience Sampling	94
Quota Sampling	95
Accidental Sampling	95
Snowball Sampling	95
Bias in Sampling	96
Sample Size	97
11. PRETESTING	**99**
Need for a Pretest or Pilot Study	99

12. DATA COLLECTION   103

    Work Schedule   103

    The Gantt Chart   104

    Bias in Information Collection   106

13. DATA PROCESSING   107

    Sorting Data   107

    Performing Quality-control Checks   108

    Processing Data   108

        Editing   108

        Categorizing   108

        Coding   109

        Summarizing   110

14. DATA ANALYSIS   111

    Introduction   **111**

    Description of Variables   **111**

    Categorical Data   112

    Numerical Data   113

        Frequency Distribution   113

        Percentages, Proportions, Ratios and Rates   116

        Diagrams and Graphs   120

    Computation of Percentages for a Frequency Table   126

        Total Percentages   127

        Column Percentages   128

        Row Percentages   128

    Cross Tabulation   **129**

Types of Cross Tabulations 129

Statistical Measures 132

Central Measures 133

    Mean 134

    Median 135

    Mode 136

    Relationship Among the Averages 137

    Correcting an Incorrect Average 139

Dispersion Measures 142

    Range 143

    Standard Deviation 144

Normal/Symmetrical Distribution 150

Population–Sample Relationship 152

Confidence Interval 153

95% Confidence Interval of Mean 153

95% Confidence Interval of Percentage 154

Correlation and Regression Analysis **155**

Correlation Analysis 155

    Types of Correlation 155

    Uses of Correlation Analysis 158

    Methods of Studying Correlation 158

    Coefficient of Determination 165

    Spearman's Rank Correlation 166

Regression Analysis 169

    Uses of Regression Analysis 170

Regression Line	171
Properties of Regression Coefficients	174
Tests of Significance	**174**
Test of Significance: *t*-test	176
Test of Significance: Paired *t*-test	182
Testing the Significance of Observed Correlation Coefficient	184
15. REPORT WRITING	187
Introduction	187
Characteristics of a Good Report	187
Format and Contents of a Research Report	188
Preliminary Section	189
Text or Body of the Report	192
Reference Material	195
Footnotes	199
Use of Footnotes	199
Footnote Contents	199
Placement and Numbering of Footnotes	200
Conventions in Footnoting	200
Editing and Evaluation	202
Evaluation of a Research Report	203
Appendix 1	*207*
Appendix 2	*209*
Appendix 3	*211*
Selected Bibliography	*213*
Index	*215*

FUNDAMENTALS OF RESEARCH

MEANING OF RESEARCH

Research, in simple words, means a search for facts—answers to questions and solutions to problems. "Research" is made up of two words—"re" and "search".

Research is a continuous and dynamic process. Research is the systematic collection, analysis and interpretation of data to answer a certain question or solve a problem. Research is a movement from the known to unknown. It is a voyage of discovery —unfolding truth by systematic scientific search for pertinent information on a specific topic. Research is considered to be a formal, systematic, and intensive process of fact finding, experimentation, analysis of data and arriving at valid conclusions. Research starts with a problem. Then it is followed by the collection of data or facts, critical analysis and decision-making based on the actual evidence. Research seeks to find explanations to unexplained phenomenon, clarify the doubtful facts and correct the misconceived facts.

PURPOSE OF RESEARCH

Research is needed to unfold the truth by systematic methods. Constant search and research are essential to know the exact truth because with the passage of time, new facts may change, the problem may undergo change and so also the concept.

A good example for research is a search for fuel for renewable energy. The main aim of research is to find out the truth which is hidden and which has not been discovered yet. Each research study has its own specific purpose.

CHARACTERISTICS OF RESEARCH

Research is a process of searching for the unknown from the known and hence research demands a clear statement of the problem. Research

- builds on the existing data, using both positive and negative findings.
- collects and organizes in such a way that they answer the research question.
- requires expertise.
- requires a plan.

A good research is mathematical in precision, accurate in research design, perfect in the use and operation of tools. Therefore, much depends on accurate data collection and in recording of observation and analysis of data with validity in conclusion. Reorganizing or restating what is already known is not research. It is not aimlessly looking for something in the hope that one will come across a solution. Many nutritional studies conducted in Third World countries revealed the prevalence of nutritional problems but not much about why and how the problem could be solved.

CHARACTERISTICS OF A RESEARCHER

Quality of the research depends upon the characteristics of the researcher too and therefore a researcher requires certain basic qualities.

- ✎ Background/subject information.

- ✎ Objectivity and logic in applying every possible test to validate the procedure employed, data collected and conclusions reached, i.e., no bias.

- ✎ Courage to face the criticism from those who have different conclusions.

- ✎ The quest for answers to unsolved problems. But replication (repetition and duplication) is also desirable to confirm or to raise questions about the conclusions of previous studies.

- ✎ Patience to carefully record and report the findings.

CLASSIFICATION OF RESEARCH

INTRODUCTION

Classification of research into different categories is not highly rigid, clear-cut and sharp. In many ways they appear to overlap one another. Research may be classified according to its major intent/purpose or the methods used.

Classification based on intent/purpose	Classification based on method
Pure research	Experimental research
Applied research	Analytical study
Exploratory research	Historical research
Descriptive research	Survey research
Diagnostic study	Case study
Evaluation study	Field studies
Action research	

PURE RESEARCH

Pure or fundamental research is conducted for the purpose of developing scientific theories, by discovering basic principles or broad generalizations of a discipline, rather than for the purpose of solving some immediate problems.

Pure research helps in

✎   developing general theories which will help in solving many practical problems.

Example

Maslow's theory of motivation serves as a guideline for formulating incentive schemes for employees in organizations.

ᕮᏉᏀᕮᏉᏀᕮᏉᏀᕮᏉᏀᕮᏉᏀ

✎   developing scientific knowledge.

Example

By applying scientific knowledge developed by pure researchers, various appliances like radio, television and computers have been invented.

ᕮᏉᏀᕮᏉᏀᕮᏉᏀᕮᏉᏀᕮᏉᏀ

Thus pure research lays the foundation for applied research.

APPLIED RESEARCH

The purpose of applied research is to improve a product or a process and to test theoretical concepts in actual problematic situations. It is mainly problem-oriented and action-directed. It seeks an immediate and practical result. Applied research helps in

1. integration of many theories and principles of various disciplines.

2. conceptual clarification by operationalizing the concepts.

3. testing the validity of existing theories.

4. contributing new facts which enrich the concerned body of knowledge.

Example

1. Marketing research is carried out to develop new marketing strategies.

2. Educational research is carried out to find new methods of teaching and learning process.

EXPLORATORY RESEARCH

It is the preliminary study of an unfamiliar problem about which the researcher has little or no knowledge. Exploratory research is necessary to get initial insight into the problem for the purpose of formulating more precise investigation. The purpose of the exploratory research is to

- make a precise formulation of the problem.
- increase the researcher's familiarity with the problem.
- identify the causes of problems.
- determine whether it is feasible to take it as a research study.

Example

To detect the possible reasons for bottlenecks in the functioning of two health centres, one can compare two health centres, one that is functioning well and the other that does not function satisfactorily.

DESCRIPTIVE RESEARCH

It is a fact-finding investigation describing, recording, analysing and interpreting conditions that exist. It helps to discover relationship between existing non-manipulated variables. It gives proper basis for understanding and solving current problems, and guides in planning and formulation of policies. Information may be collected through interviews, questionnaires or systematic direct observation. The purpose of descriptive research is to

- ✎ receive evidence concerning existing standard.
- ✎ identify norms with which to compare present conditions in order to plan for the next step.
- ✎ provide facts needed for planning social action programmes.

Several descriptive studies have helped to formulate policies in solving certain problems.

Example

Evaluation of immunization coverage among children and of useful insight of any event that occurred in the population.

DIAGNOSTIC STUDY

It is directed towards discovering what is happening, why it is happening and what can be done about it. It aims at identifying the causes of a problem and the possible solutions for it. While a descriptive study is oriented towards finding out what is occurring, a diagnostic study is directed towards discovering why it is occurring and what can be done about it. Diagnostic study is necessary in testing whether certain variables are associated. It is more actively guided by hypotheses.

Example

Identifying the factors associated with infant mortality helps to find out the causes for infant mortality.

EVALUATION STUDY

It is done for assessing the effectiveness of social or economic programmes implemented or for assessing the impact of developmental projects. Evaluative research is necessary to assess or appraise the quality and quantity of an activity and its performance, and to specify the attributes and conditions required for its success.

Example

Evaluating the impact of various rural development programmes on rural people.

ACTION RESEARCH

Action research is focused on immediate application, not on the development of theory. It is a concurrent evaluation study of an action programme launched for solving a problem or for improving an existing situation. This research is most successful in bridging the perceived gap between the practice practised and the practice desired.

Example

Change in dietary pattern can be examined before and after giving nutrition education to mothers in a village.

EXPERIMENTAL RESEARCH

Experimental research is designed to assess the effects of particular variables on a phenomenon by keeping the other variables constant or controlled. It is the blueprint of the procedures that enable the researcher to test a hypothesis by reaching a valid conclusion about the relationship between independent and dependent variables. It aims at determining whether and in what manner variables are related to each other.

A number of experimental designs are widely used only in laboratory settings. For ethical reasons, the opportunities for experiments involving human subjects are restricted. Therefore experimental designs may have to be replaced by quasi-experimental designs.

Example

The impact of chemical fertilizer and organic manure on the yield of crops can be estimated.

ANALYTICAL STUDY OR STATISTICAL METHOD

Analytical study is a system of procedures and techniques of analysis applied to quantitative data. This method is used in different fields in which numerical data are generated.

Example

A survey on malnutrition to find out the percentage of malnourished children in a certain population.

HISTORICAL RESEARCH

Historical research gives an exact knowledge of the past and enables one to interpret the future. It is the application of the scientific method of inquiry to historical problems. The main purpose of historical research is to gain a clearer perspective of the past and the present. The chief sources of data are direct and indirect uncontrolled observation with the aid of various measuring instruments and data-gathering devices and documents. The approach may be longitudinal. A systematic historical study is of immense use in understanding the past and in drawing the inferences for the present and future in the field of education, science and its application.

SURVEY RESEARCH

Survey is a method of research involving collection of data directly from a population or a sample at a particular period. The purpose of many surveys like socioeconomic surveys and marketing surveys is simply to provide information to government or business enterprises for an in-depth analysis and complex interpretations. All aspects of human behaviour, social and economic institutions can be surveyed. The survey method facilitates drawing generalizations about a large population on the basis of studies of representative sample.

CASE STUDY

A case study is an in-depth comprehensive study of a person, an episode, a programme or any social unit. A case study helps to secure a wealth of information about the unit of study which may provide clues or ideas for further research. It provides many specific details that are overlooked in other methods. It employs more techniques to gather information about a particular unit or a sample. This study has its own merits and limitations.

FIELD STUDIES

Field studies are scientific enquiries aimed at discovering the relations and interactions in social institutions and actual life situations. Field studies are concerned with a thorough knowledge of the unit under study by directly studying the processes through observation of interaction in their natural occurrence.

3
RESEARCH PROCESS

Research process consists of a series of actions or steps necessary to effectively carry out research. The research process consists of a number of closely related activities. Such activities overlap continuously as shown in Figure 3.1 rather than follow a strictly prescribed sequence. The first step determines the nature of the last step to be undertaken. The various steps involved in a research process are not mutually exclusive, nor are they separate and distinct.

The steps are interrelated and the arrows (Figure 3.1) indicate that the process is not always linear but often cyclical. However, the order of various steps provides a useful procedural guideline regarding the research process. These various processes will be individually discussed in the chapters that follow.

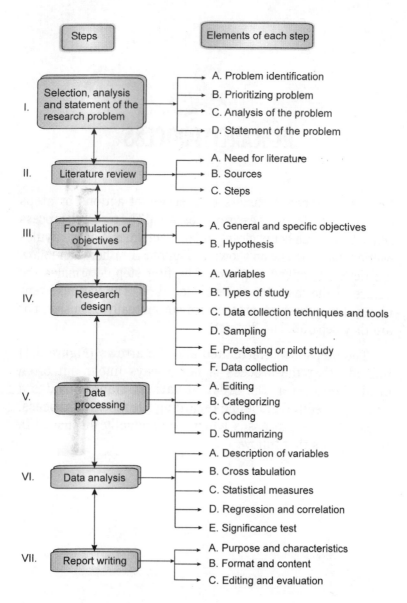

Figure 3.1   Steps and elements in research process

4
SELECTION, ANALYSIS AND STATEMENT OF THE PROBLEM

INTRODUCTION

One of the most difficult phases of any research work is the choice of a suitable problem. The researcher should not take a hasty decision. Before finalizing the research problem, several conditions have to be satisfied. A number of criteria in the form of conditions might be listed for guidance in the selection of a topic for research. Researcher's interest, competency and researcher's own resource such as finance and time also must be evaluated before selecting a research problem. A problem properly selected will enable the researcher to be on the track, otherwise it may create curdles.

PROBLEM IDENTIFICATION

After selecting the broad area for research from personal experience, professional literature, personal contact in seminars and from mass media, the researchers must narrow it down to a highly specific research problem. They must state the specific question for which they seek an answer through the application of scientific method.

It is not possible to list all the problems that need to be researched. Researchers normally select a single problem at a time because of unique needs and purposes. However, there are some important sources which are helpful to a researcher for selecting a problem.

Whether a problem situation requires research depends on the following conditions:

- ✎ There should be a difference between the existing situation and the ideal one. The reasons for this difference should not be known.

Example

The percentage of pregnant mothers going for antenatal check-up are only 60% instead of the desired 100%.

- ✎ There should be more than one possible answer or solution to the problem.
- ✎ The problem should have possibilities of empirical testing.
- ✎ There should be possibilities of getting relevant data.

Example

Is sex education necessary? This is not researchable because these questions are philosophical in nature.

- ✎ The problem should be a significant one.
- ✎ The problem should be such that the answer is not already available.

Example

"Failure to immunize pregnant mothers leads to neonatal tetanus". This will not be considered as a good problem because it has already been researched by a number of people.

✎   Management problems need not be taken up for research.

Example

Non-availability of vaccine may be a reason for immunization failure. So policy makers should ensure the supply of vaccine rather than launch a research to find out the reasons for the non-availability of vaccine. Research should be focused to find the reasons or barriers of immunization in spite of the supply of vaccines.

PRIORITIZING THE PROBLEM

Each problem that is taken for research has to be judged based on certain criteria. They are

✎   Relevance
✎   Avoidance of duplication
✎   Feasibility
✎   Political acceptability
✎   Applicability
✎   Urgency of data needed
✎   Ethical acceptability

Relevance

The topic chosen should be a priority problem. The questions to be asked in this regard include:

✎   How large or widespread is the problem?
✎   Who is affected?
✎   How severe is the problem?

If the topic is not relevant, it is not worthwhile to continue.

Avoidance of Duplication

It is important to find out whether the suggested topic has been investigated before, either within the proposed study area or in another area with similar conditions. If the topic has already been researched, the result should be reviewed to explore whether major questions that deserve further investigation remain unanswered.

Feasibility

One has to think of the resources required to carry out the study. Thought should be given first to time, equipment and money that are locally available. Where the local resources necessary to carry out the research are not sufficient, one might consider resources available at the national level. One can explore the possibility of obtaining technical and financial assistance from others.

Political Acceptability

In general, it is easier to research a topic that has the interest and support of the authorities. This will increase the chances of the results of the study being implemented. Under certain circumstances, however, one may feel that a study is required to show that the government's policy needs adjustment. If so, one should make an extra effort to involve the policy-makers concerned at an early stage, in order to limit the chances for confrontation later.

Applicability

Researchers should find out whether the recommendations from the study will be applied. This will depend not only on the blessing of the authorities but also on the availability of resources for implementing the recommendations.

Urgency

Researchers should often ask how urgently the results are needed for making a decision, which research should be done first and which can be done later.

Ethical Acceptability

One should always consider the possibility that one may inflict harm on others while carrying out research. Therefore, one has to consider important ethical issues such as

- ✎ How acceptable is the research to those who will be studied? Cultural sensitivity must be given careful consideration.

- ✎ Can we get full consent and cooperation from the research subject?

These criteria can be measured by the following rating scales.

Table 4.1 Scales for rating the research topics

Criteria	Rating scale	Marks 1 2 3
Relevance	1. Not relevant	
	2. Relevant	
	3. Highly relevant	
Avoidance of duplication	1. Sufficient information already available	
	2. Some information available but major issues not covered.	
	3. No sound information available on which to base problem solving	

(Contd.)

Table 4.1   (Continued)

Criteria	Rating scale	Marks		
		1	2	3
Feasibility	1. Study not feasible considering available resources			
	2. Study feasible considering available resources			
	3. Study highly feasible considering available resources			
Political acceptability	1. Topic not acceptable to high-level policy makers			
	2. Topic more or less acceptable			
	3. Topic fully acceptable			
Applicability	1. No chance of recommendation being implemented			
	2. Some chance of recommendation being implemented			
	3. Good chance of recommendation being implemented			
Urgency	1. Information not urgently needed			
	2. Information could be used right away but a delay of some months would be acceptable			
	3. Data very urgently needed for decision-making			
Ethical acceptability	1. Major ethical problem			
	2. Minor ethical problem			
	3. No ethical problem			
	Total			

Source   Corlien M. VarkeVisser, Indra Pathmanathan and Ann Brownlee (1991). *Designing and Conducting Health Systems Research Projects* (Ottawa, Canada.), IDRC, vol. II, Part 1, p. 34.

ANALYSIS OF THE PROBLEM

With regard to analysis of the problem one has to

- ✎ clarify the core problem—the nature, the distribution, the size and intensity.
- ✎ identify the factors that might have contributed to the problem.
- ✎ clarify the relationship between the problem and contributing factors.
- ✎ brainstorm on all possible causes contributing to the problem.
- ✎ organize the related factors together into larger categories.
- ✎ define concepts and decide on operation by giving operational definition to the concepts under study.

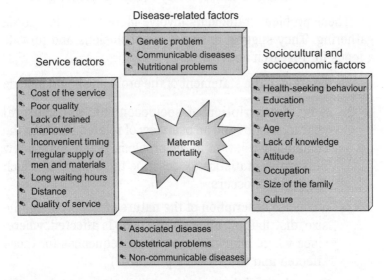

Figure 4.1   Problem analysis diagram—Factors contributing to maternal mortality

STATEMENT OF THE PROBLEM

The problem may be stated either in the form of a statement or in the form of a question. This statement provides a focus or direction to the research activity. The statement must be limited enough in scope to make a definite conclusion possible. The major statement may be followed by minor statements. Some examples of problem statement are the following.

- Children who have had kindergarten experience might demonstrate greater academic achievement in the first grade than those who have not had this experience.
- Racial segregation may have a damaging effect upon the self-image of minority-group children.
- Those who wear helmets may escape from severe head injuries.
- Deworming of children may result in weight gain.

These problem statements involve more than information gathering. They suggest answers or conclusions and provide a focus for research activity.

Description of the statement of the problem should include

- a brief description of socioeconomic and cultural characteristics and an overview of related status in the community relevant to the problem. It can include few illustrative statistics to describe the context in which the problem occurs.
- a concise description of the nature of the problem, the size, distribution, and severity (who is affected, where, since when, and what are the consequences for those affected and the services provided?)
- an analysis of the major factors that may influence the problem and a convincing argument that available knowledge is insufficient to solve it.

✎ a brief description of any solution that has been tried in the past, how well it has worked, and why further research is needed.

✎ a description of the type of information expected to result from the research and how this information will be used to help solve the problem.

✎ a short list of definitions of crucial concepts used in the statement of the problem.

The need for the study enables the researcher to systematically point out why the proposed research on the problem should be undertaken and what the researcher hopes to achieve with the outcome of the study.

REVIEW OF LITERATURE

We are living in the information era where the information is fast exchanged and new concepts are re-established and researched. Knowledge is getting doubled in a very short span of time. The researcher has to survey the available literature relating to his field of study. He must keep himself updated in his field with all available channels.

NEED FOR LITERATURE REVIEW

Reviewing the related literature helps the researcher to

- prevent duplicating work that has been done before.
- know what others have learned and reported about the problem.
- become more familiar with the various types of methodologies.
- get good background knowledge about the problem and why research is needed in that area.

SOURCES OF INFORMATION

The possible sources of information for research would be from

- individuals, groups and organizations.
- published information (books, articles, indexes, and abstract journals).

    ✎ unpublished information (other research proposals in related fields, reports, records and computer databases).

    ✎ web-based information.

STEPS INVOLVED IN COLLECTION

Steps involved in collecting the information/literature are the following.

    ✎ All researchers start with a basic knowledge in the field of research. Identify a key person who is knowledgeable on the topic and ask if he or she can give a few good references or the names of other people for getting further information.

    ✎ Look up the names of speakers on the topic at conferences who may be useful to contact.

    ✎ Contact librarians in universities, research institutions and offices and request them for relevant references on the subject.

    ✎ Examine the bibliographies and references list in key papers and books to identify relevant references.

    ✎ Look for references in indexes and abstract journals.

    ✎ Request the librarians for a computerized literature search.

References that are identified should first be skimmed or read and then summaries of the important information in each of the references should be recorded on separate index cards. These should be classified so that the information can easily be retrieved. Make sure that the references are cited correctly. Only references that relate directly to the proposed research are to be cited and discussed.

FORMULATION OF RESEARCH OBJECTIVES

The objectives of a research project summarize what is to be achieved by the study. They should be closely related to the statement of the problem.

GENERAL AND SPECIFIC OBJECTIVES

The general objective of a study states what is expected to be achieved by the study in general terms. General objective can be broken down into smaller, logically connected parts. These are normally referred to as specific objectives.

Specific objectives should systematically address the various aspects of the problem as defined under "Statement of the Problem" and the key factors that are assumed to influence or cause the problem. They should specify what will be done in the study, where, and for what purpose.

Example

The general objective is "To identify the reasons for low utilization of Anganwadi centres in the district to find out solutions". This could be broken down into the following specific objectives.

- Determining the level of utilization of the Anganwadi centres in a block in the district over the years 2001 and 2002, as compared with the target set.

- Identifying whether there are variations in utilization of centres related to the seasonal variation, types of centres and quality of services rendered.

- Identifying the factors related to the utilization of the centres.

These objectives may be divided into smaller sub-objectives focusing on

- distance between the home and the centre,

- acceptability of the services to mothers,

- quality of the services,

- identifying socioeconomic and cultural factors that may influence mothers utilizing services, and

- recommendations to all stakeholders concerning what changes should be made and how to improve the use of such centres.

Need for Objectives

Formulation of objectives helps to

- focus the study.

- avoid collection of data that are not strictly necessary for understanding and solving the problem one has identified.

- organize the study in clearly defined parts or phases.

Properly formulated, specific objectives will facilitate the development of the research methodology and will help orient the collection, analysis, interpretation and utilization of data.

Statement of Objectives

A good objective should

- ✎ cover the different aspects of the problem and its contributing factors in a coherent way and in a logical sequence.
- ✎ be clearly phrased in operational terms.
- ✎ be realistic considering local conditions.
- ✎ use action verbs that are specific enough to be evaluated. Examples of such action verbs are as follows:

1. To compare the level of utilization of the Reproductive Health Care services in various seasons of the year by the mothers.

2. To establish the pattern of utilization of Reproductive and Child Health Care (RCH) services in various seasons of the year by the mothers.

3. To verify whether increasing distance between home and health facility reduces the level of utilization of the RCH services.

4. To describe the mothers' perceptions of the quality of services provided at RCH service centres.

Researchers should avoid the use of vague and non-action verbs such as to appreciate, to understand, or to study. When the research work is evaluated, the results will be compared with the objectives. If the objectives are not spelled out clearly, it may not be possible to evaluate the research study.

HYPOTHESES

Hypothesis is a tentative solution to a problem. Hence, logically, the step that follows "formulation of the specific problems" is "derivation of hypotheses" from the problem. The problem is the question and the hypothesis is the answer. The researcher proceeds with answering the question by having a hypothesis. A hypothesis serves as a beacon that lights the way for the researcher. It predicts the relationship between one or more factors and the problem under study which can be tested. Hence hypotheses are tentative explanations of the relationship between two or more variables, and the variables must be operationally defined.

Importance of Hypotheses

Hypotheses occupy a very important place in a research. The researchers can take up a research study, particularly for analytical and experimental studies, only if they have one or more hypotheses before proceeding with their work. Hypotheses should be set up for the following reasons.

- ✎ It provides a direction to the researcher. It represents specific objectives and thus determines the type of data needed to test the proposition. Otherwise it will remain a mere supposition.

- ✎ It enables search for relevant facts only and refrains from collection of unnecessary data. Therefore it leads to economy of time and money.

- ✎ It helps the researcher to achieve more clarity in understanding the research problem.

- ✎ It provides a framework for stating the conclusions in a meaningful way.

- ✎ It helps to test whether existing theory can be used to solve the problem.

- ✎ It leads to discovery of laws.

Characteristics of a Good Hypothesis

- Clear and precise—statement should be specific, and should not be vague.
- Testable—empirically verifiable.
- Stated in simple terms.
- Amenable to testing within a reasonable time.
- Provide answer to the problem which initiated enquiring.
- Related to a body of theory—should not be a wild guess.

Types of Hypotheses

A hypothesis may be stated in a declarative form, in a null form, or in a question form.

Declarative form This is a positive form of stating.

Example

Academic achievement of extroverts is significantly higher than that of introverts.

Null form The relationship among variables is stated in a negative form. One of the objectives is to avoid personal bias of the investigator in the matter of collection of data. One can only say that a certain statement is definitely incorrect. No amount of positive confirmation of a hypothesis entails its truth.

Example

There is no significant difference between the health status of breast-fed children and bottle-fed children.

The question form The relationship among variables is stated in a question form.

Example

Will teaching the children through programmed instruction increase their test anxiety?

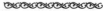

7
VARIABLES

INTRODUCTION

A research design is a logical and systematic plan prepared for directing a research study. It specifies the objectives of the study, the methodology and techniques to be adopted for achieving the objectives. It constitutes the blueprint for the collection, measurement and analysis of data. It provides a systematic plan of procedure for the researcher to follow. Research design is not a precise and specific plan to be followed without deviations, but rather a series of guide posts to keep one going in the right direction. It is a tentative plan which undergoes modifications, as circumstances demand when the study progresses.

The research design allows the researcher to make decisions regarding what, where, when, how much, and by what means. It constitutes a plan of study or study design. A research design is the arrangement of conditions for collection and analysis of data with relevance to the research purpose with economy in procedure. Research design helps the investigator to obtain answers to the questions and to control the experiment of the particular research problem under study.

A research design can be discussed under various heads—variables, types of study, data collection tools and techniques, sampling, pretesting and data collection—all of which are dealt with in seperate chapters that follow.

VARIABLES—MEANING AND TYPES

A variable is a characteristic of a person, object or phenomenon that can take on different values. Variables are the conditions or characteristics that the experimenter manipulates, controls or observes. A variable is anything that changes.

Numerical Variables

When the variables are expressed in numbers, they are called numerical variables, e.g. age in years, weight in kilograms, height in centimetres, distance in kilometres, income in rupees.

Categorical Variables

When the values of a variable are expressed in categories, they are called categorical variables.

Table 7.1   Examples of categorical variables

Variable	Categories
Colour	Red, blue, green
Staple food	Rice, maize, ragi, wheat
Sex	Male, female

Dependent and Independent Variables

The variable that is used to describe or measure the "problem under study" is called the dependent variable. The variables that are used to describe or measure the "factors" that are assumed to cause or at least to influence the problem are called independent variables.

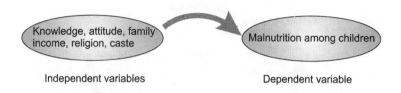

Independent variables   Dependent variable

Figure 7.1   Variables and their relationship

In Figure 7.1, malnutrition is the presumed effect and it is called dependent variable. Lack of knowledge, negative attitude, poor family income, religious restrictions and caste are the presumed causes and they are called independent variables.

Active Variables

The variables which are directly manipulated by the experiments are called active variables, e.g. method of teaching.

Attribute Variables

Attribute variables are those characteristics that cannot be altered by the experiments, e.g. age, sex, caste, religion, etc.

Composite Variables

Variables based on two or more variables may be termed as composite variables. Dental care may be measured by DMF index:

D—Number of permanent teeth that are decayed

M—Number of missing teeth

F—Number of teeth that have been filled

Confounding Variables

A variable that is associated with the problem and with a possible cause of the problem is known as confounding variable.

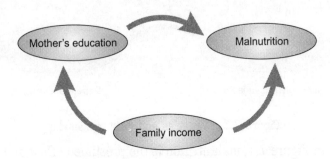

Figure 7.2 Relationship between the variables

A confounding variable may either strengthen or weaken the apparent relationship between the problem and a possible cause.

There are two types of confounding variables, (i) intervening and (ii) extraneous variables.

Intervening variables Certain factors or variables may influence the relationship even though they cannot be observed directly and they are called intervening variables, e.g. anxiety, fatigue and motivation.

Extraneous variables Extraneous variables are those uncontrolled variables that may have a significant influence upon the results of a study, e.g. age and sex.

Qualitative Variables

Qualitative variables are those which fit research subjects into categories in which the notion that one category is higher or lower than another category is meaningless, e.g. sex of a subject (whether the subject is a male or female).

Quantitative Variables

Quantitative variables are based on the notion that a subject may have more or less of a given characteristic than another subject, e.g. height, weight and intelligence test score.

Continuous Variables

A quantitative variable can take on any value over a range of values; it can also take on an infinite set of values. Such a variable is said to be a continuous variable, e.g. height, weight, spelling ability and intelligence.

Universal Variables

These are variables which are so often relevant in investigations of groups or populations, that their inclusion should always be considered. A suggested basic list of these variables include sex, age, parity, religion, marital status, social class and attributes which may be used as indicators of social class or as variables in their own right—e.g. occupation, education, income, place of residence, region, urban/rural. The background variables are often related to a number of independent variables, so that they influence the problem indirectly. Hence, they are called background variables, e.g. age, sex, educational level, socioeconomic status, marital status.

SELECTION AND STATEMENT OF VARIABLES

The variables studied should be selected on the basis of their relevance to the objectives of the study. If the objectives are formulated in writing, the key variables have to be specifically mentioned in the objectives. The more specific the formulation of objectives, the greater the number of variables to be included.

In selecting the additional variables, it is helpful to start with a list of all the characteristics that are known or suspected to affect or cause the characteristics that the investigator wants to study. The variables selected for the study should be only as many as necessary and as few as possible.

Factors are rephrased as variables. Factors are in fact variables with negative values. Variables should be formulated in a neutral way, so that they can take on positive as well as negative values. Table 7.2 presents some examples of negative "factors" and how they can be rephrased as "variables".

Table 7.2   Factors rephrased as variables

Factors	Variables
Long waiting time	Waiting time
Poor quality of services	Quality of services
Lack of supervision	Frequency of supervisory visits
Poor knowledge of maternal and child health	Knowledge on maternal and child health

When defining variables on the basis of the problem analysis, it is important to note which variables are measurable and which need indicators. Once appropriate indicators have been identified, we know what information is needed. This makes the collection of data and analysis more focused and efficient.

OPERATIONALIZING VARIABLES

After selecting the variables, variables should be explained in operational terms in terms of objectively measurable facts and stating if necessary, how these facts are to be obtained (Table 7.3). The researcher must choose a definition which will be useful to him for the purpose of the study.

There are two kinds of definitions, (i) descriptive or conceptual, and (ii) operational. Variables should be clearly defined, as the same term may have more than one meaning. Descriptive definition is often kin to a dictionary meaning, e.g. obesity may be defined as excessive fatness or as 'overweight' or as a bodily condition which is socially regarded as constituting excessive fatness as per descriptive definition.

Only when operational definitions are given, variables can be measured with precision and consistency. Operational definition is phrased in terms of objectively observable facts, and is sufficiently clear and explicit to avoid ambiguity, e.g. operational definition for obesity may be given in different ways as weight, based on weighing in under clothes and without shoes, or which exceeds by 10% more than the mean weight of persons of the subjects with same sex, age and height.

Table 7.3 A framework for defining variables

Concept	Descriptive definition	Operational definition of variables	Scales of measurement
Age	Actual age of a person in years	Age at last birthday	Months and years.
Haemoglobin level	The respiratory pigment in the RBC	Haemoglobin concentration in capillary blood, measured by haemoglobino-meter	Grams per 100 ml, rounded off to nearest gram.
Nutritional status	Condition of health influenced by the utilization of food and nutrients	Weight in relation to age compared to a standard growth curve	Well nourished—>80% of standard. Moderately nourished—60–80% of standard. Severely malnourished—<60% of standard.
Immunization coverage	The extent of children with increasing specific antibody in the tissues	Percentage of children immunized in a particular age group	High— >80%. Medium—60–80%. Low —<60%.

TYPES OF STUDY

INTRODUCTION

The type of study design chosen depends on

- the type of problem and its environment.
- the knowledge already available about the problem.
- the resources available for the study.

A good description of the problem and identification of major contributing factors often provide enough information to take action. When exploring complicated problems, we want to go further and determine the extent to which the independent variables contribute to the problem. For these types of problems, more rigorous analytical studies are to be conducted before we decide on appropriate interventions. Research studies are broadly classified into

- Non-intervention studies
- Intervention studies

In the case of non-intervention studies, the researcher just describes and analyses the researchable objects or situations but does not intervene, e.g. factors that contribute to low birth weight, factors that contribute to non-utilization of health services, etc.

In the case of intervention studies, the researcher manipulates the objects or situations and measures the outcome of his/her manipulations, e.g. by implementing intensive health education and measuring the improvement in immunization rates, interventions like giving iron and folic acid tablets to reduce the prevalence of anaemia, etc.

NON-INTERVENTION STUDIES

There are three types of non-intervention studies. They are

- Exploratory studies
- Descriptive studies
- Analytical studies

Exploratory Studies

An exploratory study is a small-scale study involving relatively a short duration, which is carried out when little is known about a situation or a problem. Comparison can also be done to identify variables that help to explain why one group of persons or objects differs from another.

Example

Two primary health centres are functioning well and two others are not. We can explore the possible reasons. We have to approach the problem from different angles at the same time. If the problem and its contributing factors are not well-defined, it is advisable to do an exploratory study before doing a descriptive or comparative study.

Descriptive Studies

Descriptive study involves systematic collection and presentation of data to give a clear picture of a particular situation. Descriptive studies can be carried out either on a small or large scale.

Descriptive case studies describe in detail the characteristics of one or a limited number of "cases." Such a study can provide a useful insight into a problem.

Cross-sectional surveys aim at quantifying the distribution of certain variables in a study population at one point of time. They may cover

- physical characteristics of people, materials or the environment, e.g. prevalence survey of diabetes, immunization coverage.

- socioeconomic characteristics of people, e.g. age, education, marital status, number of children and income.

- the behaviour of people, and the knowledge, attitudes and beliefs, and the opinions that may help to explain the behaviour.

A cross-sectional survey may be repeated to measure changes over time in the characteristics that were studied (NFHS -I, II, III). The survey may be very large with hundreds or even thousands of study units. In NFHS (National Family Health Survey), more than 4000 samples are taken in every state. If a cross-sectional study covers the total population, it is called a census.

Analytical Studies

An analytical study attempts to establish causes or risk factors for certain problems. This is done by comparing two or more groups, some of which have developed the problem and some of which have not.

Figure 8.1   Types of analytical studies

Cross-sectional studies   The cross-sectional studies focus on comparing as well as describing groups.

Example

A survey on malnutrition may wish to establish

- ✎ the percentage of malnourished children in a certain population.

- ✎ socioeconomic, physical, political variables that influence the availability of food.

- ✎ feeding practices, and the knowledge, beliefs, and opinions that influence these practices.

In any comparative study, one has to watch out for confounding or intervening variables.

Case studies   The aim of a case study is to know precisely the factors and causes which explain the complex behavioural patterns of a unit and the place of the unit in its surrounding. It gives enough information about a person or a group or a unit. Under the case study method, a subject is studied both horizontally and longitudinally. It is both an intensive and extensive study of a unit. The method may be helpful in gaining experience, in discovering new facts and in formulating valid hypotheses.

Example

A case study can be done to identify the factors responsible for the prevalence of nutritional problems among rural children. A specific number of children (four from each) may be selected among children suffering from deficiency diseases like anaemia, Kwashiorkar, vitamin A deficiency and angular stomatitis. The data on the children's nutritional history right from the time of birth to the present feeding practices can be gathered from the parents and can be supplemented by observation.

The interpretation of the case with an analytical approach will enable the investigator to cull out all predisposing factors like poor family income, large family size, short birth interval, lack of knowledge on nutrition and superstitions, and so on. From the case study, we may come out with many findings which may not be widely known as the causes for deficiency diseases because it involves an in-depth study.

Case–control studies In a case–control study, the researcher compares one group among which a problem is present with another group, called a control or comparison group, where the problem is absent, to find out what factors have contributed to the problem.

Example

Case : Children who died within the first month of life.

Control : Children who survived their first month of life.

In studying the causes for neonatal death, the researcher first selects 'cases' (children who died within the first month of life) and then 'controls' (children who survived their first month of life). He/she then interviews their mothers to compare the history of these two groups of children to determine the risk factors for the death of the infant.

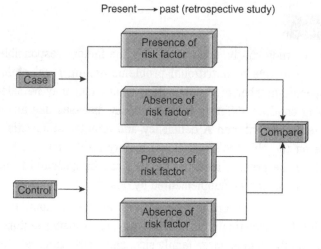

Figure 8.2   A case—control study design

Cohort studies   A group of individuals is exposed to a risk factor compared with a group of individuals not exposed to the risk factor. The researcher follows both the groups over time and compares the occurrence of the problem. It is expensive and labour-intensive.

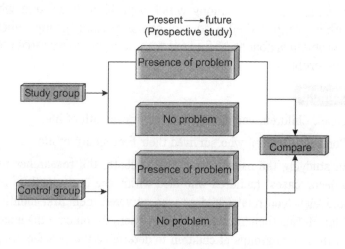

Figure 8.3   A cohort study design

Example

Study group: Smokers

Control group: Non-smokers

A good example of a Cohort study is the study of smokers and non-smokers to determine whether smoking is a risk factor for developing lung cancer. The control group should be selected at the same time as the study group, and both should be followed with the same intensity to determine whether the study group develops a higher prevalence of lung caner than the control group. Any of the three types of analytical studies may be used to investigate possible causes of a problem.

Cross-sectional studies or case–control studies are usually preferred to Cohort studies for financial and practical reasons.

Cross-sectional studies and case–control studies are relatively quick and inexpensive. With cross-sectional studies, however, the number of stratifications one can make is limited by the size of the study. The major problem with case–control studies is the selection of appropriate control groups. The matching of cases and controls has to be done with care.

Cohort studies are the only sure way to establish causal relationships. However, they take a longer time than case-control studies and are labour-intensive and, therefore, expensive. The major problems are usually related to the identification of all cases in a study population especially if the problem has a low incidence, and to the inability to follow up all persons included in the study over a number of years because of population movement.

INTERVENTION STUDIES

In the intervention studies, the researcher manipulates a situation and measures the effect of this manipulation. The two categories of intervention studies are

✎ Experimental studies

✎ Quasi-experimental studies

Experimental Studies

An experimental study is a type of study design that can actually prove causation. In an experimental study, individuals are randomly allocated to at least two groups. One group is subject to an intervention, while the other group is not. The outcome of the intervention is obtained by comparing the two groups. Experimental research is the description and analysis of what will be or will happen or occur, under carefully controlled conditions.

Experimental design is concerned with conducting experiments to find out the cause-and-effect relationship of the phenomenon under study. It is the highest stage of social research. It reduces personal bias.

A typical experimental study design has three characteristics.

✎ Manipulation—The researcher introduces some change in the intervention in one group of subjects in the study.

✎ Control—The researcher introduces one or more control groups to compare with the experimental group.

✎ Randomization—The researcher takes care to randomly assign subjects to the control and experimental groups. Each subject is given an equal chance of being assigned to either group, e.g. by assigning them numbers and blindly selecting the numbers for each group.

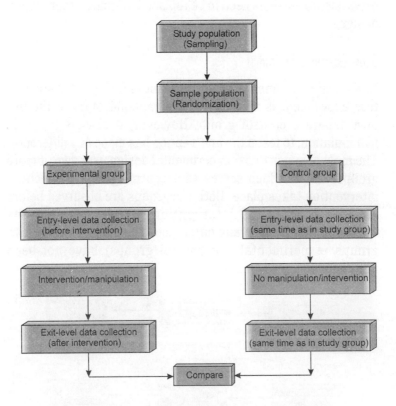

Figure 8.4 A typical experimental study design

Importance of experimental design

- ✎ Permits repetition of the investigation and verification of observation is facilitated.
- ✎ Cause-and-effect relationships are analysed with much speed.
- ✎ Permits formulation of hypothesis and rigorous check.

In real life, it is often difficult to assign persons at random to two groups, or to maintain a control group. Therefore, experimental designs need to be replaced by quasi-experimental designs.

Quasi-Experimental Studies

In a quasi-experimental study, at least one characteristic of a true experiment is missing—either randomization or the use of a separate control group. However, it always includes manipulation, to test if the intervention has made any difference. The most common quasi-experimental design uses two or more groups, one of which serves as a control group in which no intervention takes place. Both the groups are observed before as well as after the intervention, to test whether the intervention has made any difference. The subjects in the two groups (experimental and control groups) have not been randomly assigned.

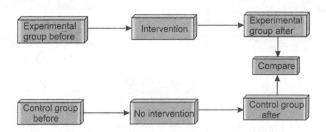

Figure 8.5   A commonly used quasi-experimental study design

Example

A researcher plans to study the effects of health education on an immunization campaign in a village. He/she decides to select one village in which health education sessions on immunization were given, and another village with no health education was included as a control. The immunization campaigns are carried out in the same manner in both villages. A survey is undertaken to determine if immunization coverage in the village where health education was introduced before the campaign is significantly different from the coverage in the "control village" which did not receive health education.

☙☙☙☙☙☙☙☙☙

Before–After Study

There is another type of design which is easy to set up by using only one group. Here only one group is chosen and the situation is analysed before and after the intervention, to test whether there is any difference in the observed problem.

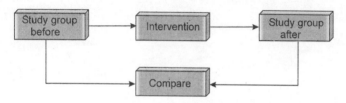

Figure 8.6 Before–after study design

Example

A primary health centre was extremely crowded and the patients were found waiting for long hours. The district health officer conducted a study to analyse the bottlenecks. They implemented the suggested reccomendations. Three months later, another study was conducted to check whether the waiting period had decreased or needed further action.

☙☙☙☙☙☙☙☙☙

This design is often used for management problems that pertain to one single unit—school, hospital, village, etc. However, if the problems occur on a large scale and if they are influenced by other factors apart from the intervention, the design should include both an experimental and control group.

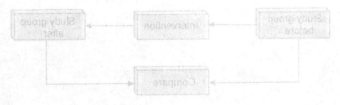

9

DATA, AND DATA COLLECTION
TECHNIQUES AND TOOLS

INTRODUCTION

Data are facts serving as the basis for research study. Data are the raw materials which the researcher has to convert into a coherent whole.

The researcher is often faced with the difficult problem of obtaining or gathering the desired information or data. Utmost care must be taken while collecting the data because data constitute the foundation on which the super structure of statistical analysis is built.

CLASSIFICATION OF DATA

Depending on the sources, data may be classified as primary data and secondary data.

Primary Data

Primary data are obtained by a study specifically designed to fulfil the objectives of the study. Such data are original in character and are generated in large number of surveys conducted by researchers and institutions.

Examples

1. Data obtained in a population census by the office of the Registrar General and Census Commissioner and Ministry of Home Affairs, GOI.

2. Family register in a Panchayat.

3. Students' register in a college/university.

Advantages

✎ The secondary source may contain mistakes due to errors in transcription, when the figures were copied from the primary source.

✎ The primary source frequently includes definitions of terms and units used.

✎ The primary source often includes a copy of the schedule and a description of the procedure used in selecting the sample and in collecting the data.

✎ The primary source usually shows data in greater detail.

Secondary Data

Data which are primary in the hands of one becomes secondary in the hands of another. Data are primary for the individual or institution collecting them whereas for the rest they are secondary.

Example

For the office of the Census Commissioner, the census data are primary, whereas for all the others who use such data, they are secondary, e.g. information from NFHS.

Advantages

✎ It is highly convenient to use information which someone else has compiled.

✎ Secondary data are much quicker to obtain than primary data.

✎ Secondary data may be available on some subjects where it would be impossible to collect primary data.

Limitations

✎ The first is the difficulty of finding data which exactly fit the need of research study.

✎ The second problem is finding data which are sufficiently accurate.

✎ The secondary source may contain mistakes due to errors in transcription, when the figures were copied from the primary source.

Choice between primary and secondary data The choice between the primary and secondary data depends mainly on the following considerations.

✎ Nature and scope of the enquiry.

✎ Availability of financial resources.

✎ Availability of time.

✎ Degree of accuracy desired.

✎ The collecting agency, i.e., whether an individual, an institution or a government body.

Precautions in the use of secondary data Secondary data should not be accepted at their face value. The reason is that such data may be erroneous in many respects, due to bias, inadequate size of the sample, substitution, errors, of definition, etc. Even if there are no errors, such data may not be suitable and adequate for the purpose of the enquiry. Hence, while using such data the researcher should consider the following aspects.

     ✎ Whether the data are suitable for the purpose of research study.

     ✎ Whether the data are adequate for the research.

     ✎ Whether the data are reliable.

Data may also be classified into two categories on the basis of the attributes or qualities of the data.

     1. Qualitative data

     2. Quantitative data

Qualitative Data

This classification includes intelligence, hard work, sex, literacy, religion, etc. Such qualitative attributes cannot be measured in terms of units of measurements. We can find only the number of people in whom these attributes are present or absent.

Example

Literacy is an attribute with which we can distinguish between literates and illiterates. In the case of each attribute, two classes are formed. This is known as simple classification. Similarly a given population may be classified into different classes on the basis of two or more than two attributes. The people in a town may be first classified on the basis of sex into male and female, then on the basis of age and education. Such classification is known as twofold classification.

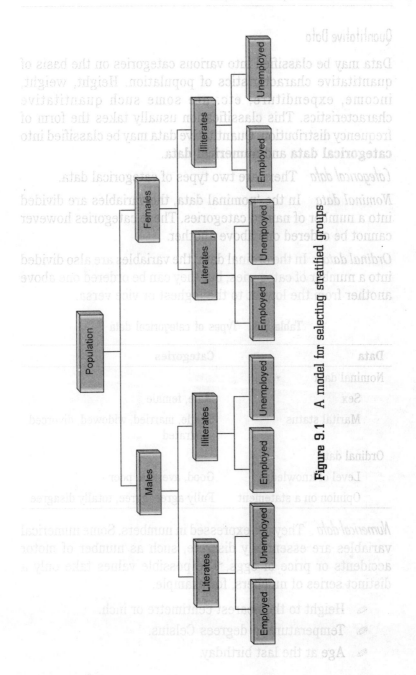

Figure 9.1 A model for selecting stratified groups

Quantitative Data

Data may be classified into various categories on the basis of quantitative characteristics of population. Height, weight, income, expenditure, etc. are some such quantitative characteristics. This classification usually takes the form of frequency distribution. Quantitative data may be classified into **categorical data** and **numerical data**.

Categorical data   There are two types of categorical data.

Nominal data   In the 'nominal data, the variables are divided into a number of named categories. These categories however cannot be ordered one above another.

Ordinal data   In the ordinal data, the variables are also divided into a number of categories, but they can be ordered one above another from the lowest to the highest or vice versa.

Table 9.1   Types of categorical data

Data	Categories
Nominal data	
Sex	Male, female
Marital status	Single, married, widowed, divorced, separated
Ordinal data	
Level of knowledge	Good, average, poor
Opinion on a statement	Fully agree, agree, totally disagree

Numerical data   They are expressed in numbers. Some numerical variables are essentially discrete, such as number of motor accidents or price of eggs. The possible values take only a distinct series of numbers, for example,

- ✎ Height to the nearest centimetre or inch.
- ✎ Temperature in degrees Celsius.
- ✎ Age at the last birthday.

But with such data, we can imagine the development of more accurate measuring instruments and greater detail in recording so that the possible recorded values increase without limit and the data become essentially continuous. In the statistical writings, such data are usually referred to as continuous.

DATA COLLECTION TECHNIQUES AND TOOLS

In the collection of data, we have to be systematic. If data are collected haphazardly, it will be difficult to answer the research questions in a conclusive way. Data collection techniques allow us to systematically collect information about our objects of study (people, objects, and phenomena) and about the settings in which they occur.

Various data collection techniques can be used such as

- using available information
- observation
- interviewing
- administering written data collection tools
- focus group discussion

USING AVAILABLE INFORMATION

There is a large body of data already collected by others, not analysed or published. Locating the sources for retrieving the information is a good starting point in any data collection effort. The researcher will have to design an instrument such as a checklist or a compilation sheet so that data can be transferred in the order in which they appear in the source document. The advantage of using existing data is that the collection is inexpensive and time is saved. However, the information may not be complete and could be out of date.

OBSERVATION

Observation is a technique that involves systematically selecting, watching, and recording the behaviour and characteristics of living beings, objects or phenomena. Observation can give additional, more accurate information on the behaviour of people. Sometimes it helps as a check on information collected.

Types of Observation, their Advantages and Disadvantages

Observation may be classified into participant observation and non-participant observation.

Participant observation The observer takes part in the situation he or she observes.

Advantages

- The group can be observed in its natural state. They are not conscious of the fact that they are being observed and consequently their behaviour is not influenced by this conscious feeling.

- The participant observer is much closer to the group than the non-participant observer, and thus, has a better insight of their doings.

- The researcher develops greater appreciation for various activities of the group.

- The participant observer can learn things that are not revealed to others because he/she actually participates with the group.

- The participant observer is generally more welcome to the group than a non-participant one.

Disadvantages

- Emotional participation of the observer kills the objectivity.

- By active participation, the researcher creates a status for themselves in the society.

- The researcher may develop familiarity with many activities through active participation. Many of them may appear common and the researcher may fail to observe them or give any importance to them.

- The range of experience is narrowed. They become a part of social hierarchy and lose contact with other groups.

- Active participation may get them entangled in many quarrels and rivalries among the people.

Non-participant observation The observer watches the situation, openly or concealed, but does not participate.

Advantages

- Objectivity and a purely scientific outlook can be maintained.

- The researcher can maintain a purely impartial status and thus can command respect and co-operation from the group.

- The researcher maintains a stranger value. Because of this, people are more willing to disclose even their weaknesses.

- It helps to observe even minute things.

- The researcher can maintain their view and keep themselves aloof from quarrels among the group.

Disadvantages

- The researcher fails to appreciate the significance of a number of actions and activities and this may make some of their findings biased in the light of their own understanding.

- They can observe only those activities that take place before them, but this forms only a small part of the whole range.

- The people fail to behave normally in front of the reseacher because they stand as critics.
- It is very difficult to digest the presence of a person who is always present to observe but never participates in anything.

Tools for Observation

The tools used in observation are

- Rating scale,
- Score-card, and
- Checklist.

Rating scale It is probably the most commonly used tool for making appraisal. Rating scale involves qualitative description of a limited number of aspects of a thing or traits of a person. Rating techniques are devices by which such judgements may be quantified. For example, one's ability to teach is rated as excellent, good, average and below average.

Advantages

- Helpful in writing reports to parents.
- Helpful in finding out the needs of students.
- Helpful in making recommendations to employees.
- Helpful in supplementing other sources of understanding about the child.
- Helpful in judging contests of various kinds such as speaking, music, etc.

Limitations

- There is difficulty in clearly defining the trait or characteristic to be evaluated.

✎ The Halo effect causes the raters to carry a qualitative judgement from one aspect to another because they have no evidence for judgement.

✎ Raters have the tendency to be too generous.

Score-card This is similar to a checklist and to a rating scale in some respects. It usually provides for an appraisal of several aspects. In addition, the presence of each characteristic or aspect, or the rating assigned to each has a pre-determined point of value. Thus, the score-card rating may yield total weighted scores that can be used in the evaluation of the object observed.

Limitations

✎ It poses difficulty in choosing, identifying and quantifying the significant aspects of the factor to be observed.

✎ There is a suspicion that the whole thing may be greater than the sum of its parts.

Checklist It is the simplest of the devices. It is a prepared list of items; the presence or absence of the item may be indicated by checking yes or no.

Advantages

✎ It is an important tool in gathering facts for educational surveys.

✎ It is used as a form for recording in observational studies of behaviour.

✎ It is used for both analysis and evaluation.

✎ It is used for checking of textbooks that deal with topics related to teaching.

✎ It is used in rating personalities.

INTERVIEWING

An interview is a data-collection technique that involves oral questioning of respondents, either individually or as a group. Answers to the questions can be recorded by writing them down or by recording their voices. Interview has been defined as a systematic method by which a person enters more or less imaginatively into the inner life of a stranger.

Purpose of Interviews

The purpose of interviews are the following.

✎ It helps secure certain information from the subject, which is known only to himself and cannot be gathered from any other source.

✎ It is a laboratory study of verbal behaviour under given circumstances.

✎ It can be used to supplement other techniques to enrich the study of persons and to check upon information gathered through other sources.

✎ It makes possible a face-to-face association and a process of inter-stimulation between the interviewer and the interviewee and this helps in securing data not obtainable by methods that do not involve an interpersonal relationship.

Kinds of Interviews

Interviews may be broadly classified as structured interviews and non-structured interviews.

Structured interviews   It is also known as controlled, guided or direct interview. In this kind of interview, a complete, detailed pre-planned schedule is used. The questions are precisely worded and systematically organized. No change is expected while interviewing the respondents.

Non-structured interviews It is also known as uncontrolled, unguided and undirected interview. No direct or predetermined questions are used in this type of interview. It is generally held in the form of free discussion or story type narrative. They are generally used in the following type of enquires.

   ✎ When pilot studies are undertaken in order to get an idea of the phenomena under study, this type of interview is used.

   ✎ This type of interview is used where reactions and feelings of the subject are to be studied pertaining to some emotional incidents, when changes in the moods and gestures are to be studied.

Non-structured interviews again can be divided into (i) focused interviews (ii) repetitive interviews (iii) depth interviews (iv) non-directive interview, and so on.

Focused interview Any specific issue, occurrence, experience or event is taken into consideration. The interviewer has the freedom to decide the manner and sequence in which the questions are to be asked. This type of interview is generally used to study the social and psychological effects of mass communication.

Repetitive interview Interview is repetitive in nature when it is desired to note the gradual influence of some social or psychological process. The repetitive interview is generally a very costly affair.

In-depth interview In-depth interview is intensive and searching in character. It is used principally for studies requiring full and detailed expressions of emotions. In-depth interview may be projective or non-projective in nature. The difference lies in the nature of the questions asked.

Non-directive interview In the case of non-directive interview, the interviewer's function is simply to encourage the respondent to talk about the given topic.

Steps in Conducting an Interview

Planning and preparing for the interview   Careful planning and preparation are necessary both in the case of structured and non-structured interviews. In both the types of interviews, the interviewer has to think of possible responses of the interviewees, and should plan the ways of dealing with inadequate responses, silences, distortions, avoidance, etc. The interviewer should be well-trained in administering the schedules and should be able to prepare an interview guide outlining subjects of study.

Establishing rapport   The basic key to successful interviewing is to establish rapport with the respondent so as to create a friendly atmosphere and put the respondent at ease. Barriers to initial communication must be overcome with patience and understanding.

Eliciting information   The interview should be carried on in an informal conversational style. The interview is a conversation with a purpose. The interviewer should ask every question given on the schedule unless there are instructions to skip it. The whole interview should be carried on in an easy, natural and relaxed manner.

Recording of responses   There are two chief means of recording the responses during the interview. If the responses are pre-coded, the interviewer needs only a check box. If the responses are open-ended, the interviewer has to record the response given verbally. For speedy recording, the interviewer should use common abbreviations.

Interpreting the interview   The interviewer should understand the objective of each question what it is trying to measure. Both the written instructions and oral training given to the interviewers should emphasize the purpose of the question and should give explanations for inadequate replies which were encountered during the pre-test. The interviewer should never suggest a possible reply.

Advantages of the interview method

✎ The information secured through interviews is likely to be more correct compared to that secured through other techniques.

✎ Scoring and test-devices can be used, the interviewer acting as experimenter. At the same time, visual stimuli to which the informant may react can be presented.

✎ Interview enables the study of an event in its emotional and historical background, and it is only in these backgrounds that real significance of an event can be followed.

✎ Through the interview method, it is possible to study even the past phenomena.

Limitations of interview   Interviews, although widely accepted as a method of social research, has the following limitations.

✎ Qualitative type interviews are sufficiently influenced by emotions and sentiments. They are not sufficiently standardized and do not provide scope for empirical verification.

✎ Interview method has a lot of subjectivity in it. What the interviewee says largely depends upon who the interviewer is. Thus, if the same person were to be interviewed by different persons, the information is most likely to show variation.

✎ Interview leaves the researcher at the mercy of the respondent. There is no source of direct observation or verification of what the respondent says.

✎ The validity of data collected through an interview is always of a doubtful character. There are a large number of sources of bias that may invalidate the information collected.

✎ Conducting an interview requires a specialized knowledge of the highest order. The interviewer must be an expert on human psychology and human behaviour and must possess a very forceful personality to prevent the interviewee from telling a lie and exaggerating facts. If not, a lot of unreliable and invalid data is collected.

ADMINISTERING WRITTEN DATA COLLECTION TOOLS

A written questionnaire can be administered through

✎ sending the questionnaire by mail with clear instructions.

✎ gathering the respondents in one place giving oral instructions, and letting the respondents fill out the questionnaires.

Questionnaires

Questionnaire is a data collection tool in which written questions are presented that are to be answered by the respondents in written form.

Characteristics of a good questionnaire

✎ It deals with an important or significant topic so that it motivates respondents to give responses.

✎ It seeks only the data which cannot be obtained from the resources like books, report, records, etc.

✎ It is as short as possible, only long enough to get the essential data.

✎ It is comprehensive and does not leave out any relevant and crucial information.

✎ It is attractive in appearance, neatly arranged and clearly printed.

✎ Directions are clear and complete, important terms are clarified, each question deals with a single idea and is worded in a simple and clear manner, and provides an opportunity for easy, accurate and unambiguous response.

✎ The questions are objective, with no clues. Suggestions are carefully avoided.

✎ Questions are presented in good psychological order proceeding from general to more specific responses.

✎ Items are arranged in categories to ensure easy and accurate responses and to help the respondent to do better justice to one category at a time.

✎ Descriptive adjectives and adverbs that have no agreed-upon meanings are avoided, for example, frequently, occasionally, etc.

✎ Double negatives are also avoided.

✎ The questions carry adequate number of alternatives.

✎ It is easy to tabulate, summarize and interpret.

✎ If mechanical tabulating equipment is to be used, it is important to allow code numbers for all possible responses to permit easy transference to machine-tabulation cards.

Advantages of using questionnaire

✎ Cost is low even when the universe is large and widely spread geographically.

✎ It is free from the bias of the interviewer, as answers are in respondent's own words.

✎ Respondents have adequate time to give well-thought-out answers.

✎ Respondents, who are not easily approachable, can also be reached conveniently.

✎ Large samples can be made use of and thus the results can be made more dependable and reliable.

Limitations of using questionnaire

✎ Low rate of return of the duly filled-in questionnaires.

✎ Bias due to non-response is often indeterminate.

✎ It can be used only when the respondents are educated and cooperative.

✎ The control over questionnaire may be lost once it is sent.

✎ There is in-built inflexibility because of the difficulty in amending the approach once questionnaires have been dispatched.

✎ There is also the possibility of ambiguous replies or omission of replies altogether to certain questions: interpretation of omissions is difficult.

✎ It is difficult to know whether willing respondents are truly representative.

✎ This method is likely to be the slowest of all.

Types of questionnaires Questionnaires are of the following types.

 i. Structured questionnaire

 ii. Non-structured questionnaire

 iii. Closed-form questionnaire

 iv. Open-ended questionnaire

Structured questionnaire It contains definite, concrete and pre-ordinate questions to elicit a more detailed response.

Non-structured questionnaire This is often known as interview guide and is used for focused, depth and non-directive interviews. It contains definite subject matter areas, the coverage of which is required during the interview.

Closed-form questionnaire It offers a list of possible options or answers from which the respondents must choose.

Example

Have you taken a health checkup? Yes☐ No☐

Advantages

✎ Answers can be recorded quickly.

✎ Analysis is easy.

Disadvantages

✎ Closed questions are less suitable for face-to-face interviews with non-literates.

✎ Respondents may choose options which they would not have thought of themselves.

✎ Important information may be missed if it is not asked.

✎ The respondents and interviewer may lose interest after a number of closed questions.

Open-ended questionnaire They permit free responses that should be recorded in the respondent's own words. The respondents are not given any possible answers to choose from, e.g. What do you think are the reasons for a high dropout rate in villages?

Advantages

✎ Issues not precisely thought of when planning the study may be explored, thus providing valuable new insights into the problem.

✎ Information provided spontaneously is likely to be more valid than answers suggested in options from which the informant must choose.

✎ Information provided in the respondent's own words may be useful as an example or illustration that adds interest to the final report.

Disadvantages

✎ Skilled interviewers are needed to get the discussion started and focused on relevant issues and to record all important information.

✎ Analysis is time-consuming and requires experience.

Schedule

Schedules are filled in by an interviewer by asking a set of questions in a face-to-face situation with another person.

Characteristics of a good schedule

✎ Accurate communication should be there; questions should be properly worded.

✎ Technical terms and ambiguity should be avoided.

Advantages

✎ It provides opportunity to establish rapport, explain the purpose and make the meaning of the items clear.

✎ It economizes on expenditure of time and money and provides more complete and usable returns.

✎ Schedule helps as an aide-memoire—the researchers have formerly prepared questions, so if they forget they can refer to the schedule.

✎ Helps in classification and analysis of data in a scientific manner.

Disadvantages

✎ The researcher is unable to contact personally all the respondents.

✎ This method requires trained enumerators to fill up schedule.

✎ The enumerators should be honest, sincere, hard working and should have patience and perseverance.

✎ The enumerators should have the capacity of cross-examination to find out the truth.

Kinds of schedules Based on the use to which they are put, schedules are classified into four types. They are

   i. Observation schedule

   ii. Rating schedule

   iii. Document schedule

   iv. Interview schedule

Observation schedule They are used for observation purposes. They contain specific topics upon which the observer has to concentrate and the nature of information that has to be recorded. Such schedules make the observation more pointed and accurate by pointing clearly what is to be observed, and how it is to be recorded.

Rating schedule They are used in those cases where the attitude or opinion is to be measured. Different ranks or scales are constructed for this purpose.

Document schedule These schedules are used for recording data from written documents like autography, case history, and diary or official records maintained by the government. Such schedules are used for preparing the source list of collecting preliminary information about the universe.

Interview schedule They are used for interview purposes. They contain standard questions that the interviewer has to ask, and blank tables that he/she has to fill up after getting information from the respondents.

Construction of a schedule

- The investigator should have a proper knowledge about the problem and should know what information he/she needs for a valid and accurate generalization on each problem.
- The questions should be complete and precise.
- The schedule should be well planned and short with proper margins.
- The questions should cover all relevant aspects of the problem.
- The questions should be in a well-ordered series.
- The schedule should be tested on a sample population.
- Printing or typing should be well spaced and easy to read.
- If necessary, pictures can be used along with the questions.

Table 9.2 Differences between a questionnaire and schedule

Questionnaire	Schedule
Sent through mail to the informants to be answered, as specified in a covering letter, without further assistance from the sender.	Generally filled out by the research worker who can interpret questions when necessary.
Observation is not possible through questionnaire.	Along with schedules, observation method can also be used.
Non-response is usually high in this case.	Non-response is generally very low.
It is not always clear as to who replies.	Identity of respondent is known.
This method is likely to be very slow since many respondents do not return the questionnaires in time.	The information is collected well in time as they are filled by the enumerators.

(Contd.)

Table 9.2 (Continued)

Questionnaire	Schedule
Personal contact is generally not possible.	Direct personal contact is established with the respondent.
This method can be used only when respondents are literates and co-operative.	This method can be used even when the respondents happen to be illiterates.
Wider and more representative distribution of sample is possible.	It is difficult to send enumerators over a relatively wider area.
Risk of collecting incomplete and wrong information is relatively more.	The information collected is generally complete and accurate.
The success of this method lies more on the quality of the questionnaire.	The success depends much upon the honesty and competence of enumerators.
In order to attract the attention of respondents, the physical appearance of questionnaire must be quite attractive.	This is not needed in the case of schedules.
Data collection is relatively cheap and economical.	Relatively more expensive. Money has to be spent on training and appointing enumerators.

Attitude Scales

They are the tools designed to measure attitudes of a subject towards issues, institutions and groups of people.

Characteristics of an attitude scale

- It provides for quantitative measure to assess the intensity of an attitude of an individual.
- It uses statements from the extreme positive position to extreme negative position.

✎ It generally uses a five-point scale—Strongly Agree (SA), Agree (A), Undecided (U), Disagree (D) and Strongly Disagree (SD). The individual gets the score as the sum of items credits.

✎ It may require the judges to pile up the given statements and compute the scale values according to the percentage of judges who place each statement in different categories. It gives the individual a score on the basis of the median scale values of the statements.

✎ It is usually standardized and norms are worked out.

✎ It disguises the attitude rather than directly asking about the attitude on the subject.

Methods of measuring attitudes   Two popular and useful methods of measuring attitudes (indirectly), which are commonly used for research purposes are:

1. Thurston technique of scaled values.

2. Linker's method of summated ratings.

Thurston technique   The procedure is fairly simple. A large number of statements, usually twenty or more, are gathered that express various points of view towards a group, institution, idea or practice. They are then submitted to a panel of judges, each of whom arrange them in eleven groups ranging from one extreme to another in position.

This sorting by each judge yields a composite position for each of the items. When there has been marked disagreement among the judges in assigning a position to an item, that item is discarded. For items that are retained, each is given its median scale value between one and eleven as established by the panel.

The list of statements are then given to the subjects who are asked to check the statement with which they agree.

The median value of the statements that they check establishes their score, or quantifies their opinion.

Advantages

✎ It is used for developing differential scales which are utilized to measure attitudes towards varied issues like war, religion, etc.

✎ It is considered more appropriate and reliable when used for measuring a single attitude.

Disadvantages

✎ High cost and effort is required to develop this attitude scale.

✎ It is not completely objective; it ultimately involves a subjective decision process.

✎ Other scale designs give more information about the attitudes in comparison to differential scale.

Linker's method This method uses items worded for or against the proposition, with five-point rating response indicating the strength of the respondents' approval or disapproval of the statement. It is designed to measure the intensity with which an attitude is expressed. The first step is the collection of a number of statements about the subject in question. Statements may or may not be correct but they must be representative of the opinion held by a substantial number of people. They must express definite favourableness or unfavourableness to a particular point of view. The number of favourable and unfavourable statements should be approximately equal. A trial test may be administered to a number of subjects. Only those items that correlate with the total test should be retained.

This scaling technique assigns a scale value to each of the five responses. All favourable items are scored from the maximum to the minimum and those opposing the proposition would be scored in the opposite order. The total of these scores on all the items measures the respondent's favourableness towards the subject in question.

If a scale consists of 30 items, the following score values will be of interest:

$30 \times 5 = 150$—most favourable attitude.

$30 \times 3 = 90$—a neutral attitude.

$30 \times 1 = 30$—most unfavourable attitude.

The summed up score of any individual will fall between 30 and 150. Item analysis is to be carried out to decide the best statements for the final scale. Items in the final scale have no scale values. All items have equal weights.

Advantages

- It is relatively easier to construct than a Thurston scale.

- This type is considered more reliable because the respondents answer each statement included in the instrument. It also provides more information and data than the Thurston-type scale.

- Each statement included here is given an empirical test for discriminating ability and as such, unlike Thurston-type scale, the Likert-type scale permits the use of statements that are not manifestly related to the attitude being studied.

- Linker-type scale can easily be used in respondent-centred and stimulus-centred studies.

Disadvantages

- With this scale, we can measure or examine whether the respondents are more or less favourable to a particular topic, but we cannot tell how much more or less they are.

✎ Often the total score of an individual respondent has little clear meaning since a given total score can be secured by a variety of answer patterns.

FOCUS GROUP DISCUSSION

A focus group discussion is a group discussion of 6–12 persons guided by a facilitator, during which group members talk freely and spontaneously about a certain topic. The purpose of a focus group discussion is to obtain in-depth information on concepts, perceptions and ideas of the group. A focus group discussion aims to be more than a question–answer interaction. The idea is that group members discuss the topic among themselves.

Participants should be roughly of the same socioeconomic group or have a similar background in relation to the issue under investigation. Communication and interaction during the focus group discussion should be encouraged in every way possible. There should be a written list of topics to be covered. One of the members of the research team should act as a facilitator for the focus group and one should serve as a recorder. The participants should be invited at least one or two days in advance and the purpose of focus group discussion should be explained. The number of focus group sessions to be conducted depends upon the project needs, resources and whether new information is still coming from the sessions.

IMPORTANCE OF COMBINING DIFFERENT DATA COLLECTION TECHNIQUES

A skilful use of a combination of different techniques can maximize the quality of the data collected and can reduce the chance of bias. One should combine both flexible and less-flexible techniques. Examples of flexible techniques are

✎ loosely structured interviews with open-ended questions

✎ focus group discussions and

✎ participant observation.

They are also called qualitative research techniques. They produce qualitative information, which is often recorded in a narrative form. Qualitative research techniques involve the identification and exploration of a number of often related variables that give an insight into the nature and causes of certain problems, and into the consequences of those problems for those affected.

A structured questionnaire that enables the researcher to quantify answers to questions, is an example of quantitative research techniques. The answer to questions can be counted and expressed numerically. Quantitative research techniques are used to quantify the size, distribution and association of certain variables in a study population—both quantitative and qualitative research techniques are often used within a single research study.

CHARACTERISTICS OF A RESEARCH TOOL

A research tool should possess the following characteristics

    i. Reliability
   ii. Validity
  iii. Practicability
  iv. Objectivity

Reliability

It refers to the consistency of the test. A good test should give more or less the same results whenever it is administered. The reliability of a test refers to the consistency of the scores obtained by the same individual on different occasions or by different individuals on different occasions. Reliability is also known as reproducibility or repeatability. For example, X-ray is a reliable test because it gives the same diagnosis even when it is used by different doctors.

Factors influencing reliability

Length of the test The longer test is more reliable than the shorter ones and there should be considerable number of tests.

Objectivity in scoring A test which can be scored objectively can give more reliable results than other methods of scoring.

Clarity of instructions If the instructions are ambiguous, different people are likely to interpret them differently and hence different answers will be obtained. Hence the instructions should not be ambiguous.

Methods of determining reliability

Reliability can be determined by the following methods:

- Test and re-test method
- Equivalent form method
- Split-half method

Test and re-test method Here the same tool is administered to a group of subjects twice at an interval of 2 to 4 weeks and the two sets of scores are correlated.

Equivalent form method Two very similar forms of the same instrument are administered to a group of subjects and the scores are compared or correlated.

Split-half method Here the instrument is divided into two equal and comparable parts and the sets of scores are correlated.

Validity

This refers to the quality of the test—measuring what it wants to measure, intends to measure and serving the purpose for which it was constructed. Validity refers to the truthfulness of a test and the degree to which the test actually succeeds in measuring what it wants or intends to measure.

Example

If a researcher is interested in measuring the IQ but performs a test that measures general knowledge, we cannot say the result is valid.

Types of validity

Face validity   This type refers to whether the given test appears to or seems to measure what it wants to measure. This type of validity does not refer to what the test actually measures.

Content validity   This type should cover the contents taught and also should cover the objectives of the subject matter. Equal weightage to both should be given.

Construct validity   This type is used by the experts who deal with psychological areas such as intelligence, personality, etc. It is used in tests that are used to study formation of various habits, skills and the like.

Predictive validity   This determines the future success of a test. The given test scores are correlated with the data collected at a future date. A student in a class is given a test and his performance will be compared with his achievement later.

Concurrent validity   This type of validity is used to indicate the validity of a new test by correlating it with a present source of information. This source of information can be obtained either immediately before or after a new test is given.

The concepts of validity and reliability are shown in Figure 9.2.

Neither valid nor reliable   Reliable but not valid

Fairly valid but not very reliable   Valid and reliable

Figure 9.2 Concepts of validity and reliability. Neither valid nor reliable—the aim does not hit the centre of the target nor do repeated attempts hit the same spot. Reliable but not valid—the aim does not hit the centre of the target (i.e. not valid) but repeated attempts do hit almost the same spot. Fairly valid but not very reliable—the aim is fairly close to the centre of the target (fairly valid) but repeated attempts do not hit the same spot, some are to the left, some to the right , etc. (not reliable). Valid and reliable—the aim hits the centre of the target and repeated attempts hit the same spot.

Practicability

This means the extent to which the test can be used practically taking into consideration the following factors:

 i.   *Ease of administration*

   ✎ The test should be conducted easily by anybody.

   ✎ Instructions should be easily understood by the pupils and the teacher.

   ✎ Should be clear, precise and definite.

ii. *Ease of scoring*

✎ Scheme of scoring should be simple, should be valued quickly and objectively.

✎ Scoring key is to be prepared.

iii. *Ease of interpretation* The test should be accompanied by complete norms. Norms are standards set for the test in terms of age, grade or class duration of time to which the subject matter has to be studied by pupils, and the area from which they are coming, urban or rural.

iv. *Economy of cost, time and energy*

✎ Testing device should not be very expensive.

✎ Time spent on it should be minimum.

✎ It should not be a very sophisticated instrument needing help of experts.

✎ Should be easily constructed, administered and interpreted with lesser amounts of money, time and energy.

Objectivity

✎ The test should not permit personal bias of the examiners to influence the scores.

✎ There should be only one correct answer.

✎ No disagreements as to what the correct answer is. If a test is to be objective, it should give more or less same or consistent results.

When administered to groups of students who belong to the same age and class. However, cent per cent objectivity is only relative and never absolute.

SAMPLING

INTRODUCTION

Sampling involves the selection of a number of study units from a defined study population. The study population has to be clearly defined, e.g. age, sex and residence. Apart from persons, study population may consist of villages, institutions, records, etc. Each study population consists of study units. Study population and study units depend on the problem to be investigated.

Some studies involve only a small number of people and thus, all of them can be included. However, research often focuses on a large population. So, for practical reasons, it is possible to include only some of its members in the investigation. Then a sample has to be drawn from the total population. Care should be taken to draw a sample in such a way that it is representative of that population in all the important characteristics. Thus, sampling may be defined as the selection of some part of an aggregate or totality on the basis of which a judgement or inference about the aggregate or totality is made for the study.

ADVANTAGES OF SAMPLING

Sampling method has certain definite advantages over census method. The advantages are as follows:

- **Saving of time**   Comparatively a smaller number of units is studied using sampling method, and naturally it requires less time than the census method.

- **Saving of money**   Survey of smaller number of cases not only requires less time, but also requires less money.

- **Detailed study**   When the number of units is large, detailed study is not possible. This is possible only when the number of cases to be studied is small.

- **Accuracy of results**   A proper sample ensures the standard of accuracy desired. Techniques have been successfully evolved to calculate the sampling error by means of statistical methods.

- **Administrative convenience**   A small sample is usually more convenient from the administrative point of view. A small sample is, therefore, more manageable especially in social research.

DISADVANTAGES OF SAMPLING

The following are the major disadvantages of sampling.

- **Chances of bias**   A bias in the sample may be caused by faulty selection of sampling method.

- **Difficulties of a representative sample**   The results of sampling are accurate and usable only when the sample is a representative of the whole study population.

- **Need for specialized knowledge**   In the absence of specialized knowledge, the researcher may commit untold blunders and the entire findings may be reduced to a useless heap.

- **Impossibility of sampling**   Sometimes, the universe is too small or too heterogeneous. In these cases, when a very high standard of accuracy has to be maintained, the sampling method is unsuitable, because even in the most accurate method of sampling, there are always some chances of error.

ESSENTIALS OF SAMPLING

The essential features of sampling include the following.

- ✎ Representativeness—a sample should be selected in such a manner that it really represents the universe.

- ✎ Adequacy—the size of the sample selected should be adequate and sufficient to represent the population.

- ✎ Independence—all items of the population should have the same chance of being selected in the sample.

- ✎ Homogeneity—there should be no basic difference in the nature of units of the universe and that of the sample.

- ✎ Accuracy—an accurate sample is one which exactly represents the population.

SAMPLING TECHNIQUES

The respondents selected should be as representative of the total population as possible in order to produce a miniature cross section. The selected respondents constitute what is technically called a "sample" and the selection process is called "sampling technique".

The selection of a sampling technique depends upon the nature of the problem, size of the universe, size of the sample, availability of finance, time, etc.

The sampling methods are of two types.

Table 10.1   Sampling methods

Probability sampling	Non-probability sampling
Simple random sampling	Judgement sampling
Stratified random sampling	Convenience sampling
Systematic random sampling	Quota sampling
Multi-stage sampling	Accidental sampling
Cluster sampling	Snowball sampling

PROBABILITY SAMPLING

Probability sampling involves random selection procedures to ensure that each unit of the sample is chosen on the basis of chance. All units of the study population should have an equal or at least a known chance of being included in the sample.

Simple Random Sampling

In a simple random selection, every member of the population has an equal chance of being included in the sample. To select a simple random sample, one needs to

- make a numbered list of all the units in the population from which one wants to draw a sample.
- decide on the size of the sample.
- arrange the units alphabetically, numerically or geographically.
- make use of either a lottery system or a table of random numbers.

We can select the digits at random from Tippet's tables of numbers. Tippet selected 10,400 digits from census reports and combined them by fours so as to give 20,400 four figure numbers. These numbers have been tested for their randomness.

Limitations

- If the area of investigation is very small, results of random sampling method cannot be applied.

- Sampling method cannot be used if the universe is heterogeneous in character.

- If the investigator is biased, the results cannot be relied upon.

Assumptions underlying random sampling

- Sample should remain the same throughout the investigation, i.e., localities once selected should not be changed.

- Each unit in the universe should have an equal chance of being included in the sample.

Example

A simple random sample of 50 students is to be selected from a school of 250 students. Using a list of all 250 students, each student is given a number (1 to 250) and these numbers are written on small pieces of paper. All the 250 papers are folded and put into a box. After the box is shaken vigorously to ensure randomization, 50 papers are taken out of the box and the numbers are recorded. The students belonging to these numbers will constitute the sample.

Merits

- It is easy to analyse data and to compute errors.

- Samples selected are representative.

- It economizes time and money.

Demerits

✎ It cannot be applied where some units of the universe are so important that their inclusion in the sample is necessary.

✎ If the sample is not large enough, it may not be representative of the population.

Stratified Sampling

This method ensures sampling in proportion to the size of the segment in the universe and reflects in a better way the characteristics of the universe. This is known as stratified sampling method.

This procedure may be good if there is no variation within each stratum.

Example

In selecting residents from urban and rural areas or of different age groups, the sampling frame must be divided into groups or strata, according to these characteristics. Random or systematic samples of a pre-determined size will then have to be obtained from each group (stratum). We can use the proportionate size in selecting the sampling units. In a proportionally stratified sampling, the number of items drawn from each stratum is proportional to the size of the strata.

To illustrate it, let us suppose that we want a sample size of 100 students to be drawn from a strength of 5000 students from five strata based on their programmes. Adopting proportional allocation, we can get the sample size from different programmes, as given in the following table.

Programme	Strength	Sample size
UG I	1500	30–100 (1500/5000)
UG II	1250	25–100 (1250/5000)
UG III	1000	20–100 (1000/5000)
PG I	750	15–100 (750/5000)
PG II	500	10–100 (500/5000)
	5000	100

Thus the sample size is in proportion to the sizes of the strata.

Merits

- It can be used when the study population is not homogeneous.
- More representative and accurate—as every unit in the strata has an equal chance of being selected.
- There is only a lesser chance of failure.
- Ensures proportional representation.
- Characteristics of each stratum can be estimated.

Demerits

- It requires accurate information to form strata.
- Separate frame for each stratum has to be prepared.

Systematic Sampling

In systematic sampling, sample units are chosen at regular intervals (e.g. every fifth) from the sampling frame. Randomly select a number to start selecting individuals from the list by blindly picking one out of twelve pieces of paper, number 1 to 12. If number 6 is picked then every twelfth student will be included in the sample, starting with student number 6, until hundred students are selected. The number selected would be 6, 18, 30, 42, etc.

For selecting additional units at evenly spaced intervals in a class of 100 students, sample of students to be selected would be 10.

Sampling fraction is given by 10/100 = 1/10, therefore sampling interval is 10. Selection of first student is randomly done between 1 and 10.

Merits

✎ It is easy to select the sample.

✎ The sample is spread over the entire population.

✎ It is easy to check the sample.

Demerits

✎ The enumerators can exercise their personal choice while arranging the units in some order.

✎ If the units undergo any change, it must be duly accounted for, otherwise the results will not be reliable.

Multi-Stage Sampling

In the multi-stage sampling, the population is distributed into a number of first-stage sampling units, and a sample is taken from these first-stage units by some suitable method. This is the first stage of sampling process. Each of these selected first sample units, is further subdivided into second-stage units, and from these, again a sample is taken by some suitable method. Further stages may be added if necessary.

Example

In the first stage, a city may be divided into a number of homogeneous regions. In the second stage, these regions may be divided into smaller wards/divisions, and in the third stage, equal number of sample may be selected randomly from each ward.

In this way, selection of a sample is made in several stages, and in each stage random sampling is adopted.

Merits

✎ It covers a large area.

✎ It cuts down the cost of preparing the sampling frame.

Demerit   Sampling error will be maximum.

Cluster Sampling

In this method, random selection is made of groups of individuals who form a cluster, and for taking a sample of three names from groups, selection may be made at random.

Example

Visiting people who are scattered over a large area may be too time-consuming. However, when a list of groupings of study units is available (e.g. villages or schools), the sample can be easily studied. A number of these groupings can be randomly selected.

Merits

✎ It cuts down the preparation of sampling frame.

✎ It cuts down the travel expenses within selected units.

Demerits

✎ If the sampling structure contains similar persons, sampling error will be there.

✎ A large number of small clusters is preferable to a small number of large clusters.

NON-PROBABILITY SAMPLING

Selection is partially subjective and does not provide every item of the universe to have an equal chance of selection. A few non-probability sampling techniques are briefly mentioned here.

Judgement Sampling

Based on the judgement of the researcher, the sample units are selected under this method. It is again known as purposive or deliberate sampling. Samples are designed to be representative.

Merit   Relevant samples can be included. The researcher can include certain stratification in the sample.

Demerit   The sample may have personal bias of the researcher. We cannot determine the sampling error.

Convenience Sampling

Convenience sampling is a method in which the sample units are selected as per the convenience of the researcher.

Example

If the researcher wants to study the attitude of villagers towards family-planning services provided by the MCH clinic, he/she decides to interview all adult patients who visit the out-patient clinic during one particular day. This is more convenient than taking a random sample of people in the village, and it gives useful first impressions.

Merit   This can be used for pilot studies.

Demerit   It is prone to bias.

Quota Sampling

Under this sampling method, quota is set up according to some special characteristics such as income groups or age groups. Within each group, the researcher is free to select the sample required.

Example

The interviewer may be asked to get samples of 5 males of 35 years of age, 2 police constables, 5 persons with an income of Rs. 4000 or over, and so on. The actual selection of members to be included in the sample is left to the discretion of the interviewer.

Merits

✎ It reduces the cost of preparing the sampling frame.

✎ It permits the researcher to substitute one person for another, in case of refusal.

Demerit As the method is prone to bias, it cannot estimate sampling error.

Accidental Sampling

The researcher selects the sample units that they come across on a street, for example, interviews conducted by T.V. reporters. It may be correct or incorrect.

Snowball Sampling

This is a technique of building up a list or a sample of a special population by using an initial set of its members as informants.

Example

If the researcher wants to study the problems of single-parent families, i.e., husband living abroad, they can ask the samples in hand to supply the names of others known to them and continue this procedure to get the needed number of samples.

Merit   It is useful for smaller populations for which no frames are readily available.

Demerit   Sample depends on the subjective choice of the original selected respondents.

BIAS IN SAMPLING

Bias in sampling is the systematic error in sampling procedures that leads to a distortion in the results of the study. There are several ways to deal with the problem and to reduce the possibility of bias:

- ✎ Data collection tools (including written introduction for the interviewers to use with potential respondents) have to be pretested. If necessary, adjustments should be made to ensure better cooperation.

- ✎ If non-response is due to absence of the subjects, follow-up of non-respondents may be considered.

- ✎ If non-response is due to refusal to cooperate, an extra separate study of non-respondents may be considered to discover to what extent they differ from respondents.

- ✎ Another strategy is to include additional people in the sample, so that non-respondents who were absent during data collection can be replaced.

SAMPLE SIZE

There is a widespread belief among researchers that the bigger the sample, the better the study results. This is not necessarily true. It is much better to increase the accuracy of the data collection than to increase the sample size. It is better to get a representative sample than a very large sample. The desirable sample size is determined by the expected variation in the data. The more varied the data, the larger the sample size needed to attain the same level of accuracy. The desirable sample size also depends on the number of cells intended in the cross tabulations. A rough guideline is to have at least 20 to 30 study units per cell.

If we include many variables in the study, the sample size should be relatively small. If there are only a few variables, we can have a larger sample.

The eventual sample size is usually a compromise between what is desirable and what is feasible.

Feasible sample size is determined by the availability of resources such as

- Time
- Manpower
- Money
- Transport and other logistics

To determine desirable sample size, there are a few general rules.

- Sample size depends on the expected variation in the data.
- The more varied the data are, the larger the sample size needed.
- Sample size depends on the number of cells in the cross tabulations.

11
PRETESTING

A **pretest** usually refers to a small-scale trial of a particular research component. A **pilot study** is the process of carrying out a preliminary study, i.e., going through the entire research procedure with a small sample.

NEED FOR A PRETEST OR PILOT STUDY

A pretest or pilot study serves as a trial run that allows us to identify potential problems in the proposed study. Although this means extra effort at the beginning of the research study, a pretest or pilot study enables one, if necessary, to revise the methods and logistics of data collection before starting the actual fieldwork. As a result, a good deal of time, effort and money can be saved in the long run. Pretesting is simpler and less time-consuming and economical rather than conducting an entire pilot study. The checklist given in Table 11.1 can be used while doing the pilot study.

Table 11.1 Summary of points to assess during a pretest or pilot study

Points to be assessed	Acceptable	Not acceptable	Suggestions
Reaction of respondents			
Availability of respondents			
Working hours of respondents			
Willingness of respondents			
Acceptability of the questions			
Clarity of the language used			
Data collection tools and techniques			
Tools that provide valid and reliable information			
Presentation of questions			
Format of questionnaire			
Accuracy of translation			
Categorization of questions			
Handling of the tools			
Time taken for administering tools			

Sampling procedure
Procedure to select the sample
Time needed to locate the sample
Schedule for research activities
Period allotted for data collection
Mode of transport
Sequence of activities
Data processing and analysis
Use of data master sheets
Computer entry
Data quality-control checks
Appropriateness of statistical tests
Ease of data interpretation

DATA COLLECTION

A plan for data collection can be made in two steps.

- Listing the steps that have to be carried out, making a rough estimate of the time needed for the different parts of the study and identifying the most appropriate period for data collection.

- Scheduling the different activities that have to be carried out in a work plan.

WORK SCHEDULE

A work schedule is a table that summarizes the tasks to be performed in a research project, the duration of each activity and the staff responsible.

The work schedule may include

- the tasks to be performed; each task should begin and be completed.

- the research team—research assistants and support staff to be assigned to the tasks.

- person-days required by the research team to complete the research project.

THE GANTT CHART

The Gantt chart (Table 12.1) is a planning tool which depicts graphically the order in which various tasks must be completed and the duration of each activity.

The Gantt chart indicates

✎ the tasks to be performed,

✎ who is responsible for each task, and

✎ the time each task is expected to take.

The length of each task is shown by a bar that extends over the number of months the task is expected to take.

The first draft of the work plan should be prepared when the research study is being developed. A more detailed work plan should be prepared after the pretest in the study area.

A plan for data collection should be developed so that the researcher will have a clear overview of what tasks have to be carried out and the duration of these tasks. It is always advisable to slightly overestimate the period needed for data collection to allow for unforeseen days. Timing of data collection will be determined by the accessibility and availability of the sample population.

It is extremely important that the data collected should be of good quality, that is, reliable and valid. Good rapport with the sample facilitates in getting correct information.

Table 12.1 Gantt chart

Activity	Months								Remarks
	May	June	July	Aug	Sept	Oct	Nov	Dec	
Selection of the study	▓								
Review of literature		▓							
Research design		▓	▓						
Finalization				▓					
Pretesting				▓	▓				
Data collection					▓	▓			
Analysis						▓	▓		
Report writing							▓	▓	
Final report								▓	

BIAS IN INFORMATION COLLECTION

Bias in information collection is a distortion that results in the information not being representative of the true situation. Bias during data collection may be due to

- ✎ questionnaires with fixed or closed questions on topics about which too little is known.
- ✎ open-ended questions without guidelines on how to ask them.
- ✎ vaguely phrased questions or questions placed in an illogical order.
- ✎ there is a risk that the researcher will see or hear only things in which he or she is interested and will miss information that is critical to the research.
- ✎ the respondents may mistrust the intention of the interview and dodge certain questions or give misleading answers. Such bias can be reduced by introducing the purpose of the study to the respondents.

By being aware of such potential bias, it is possible to prevent it to a certain extent.

13
DATA PROCESSING

The plan for processing of data must be prepared before the data is collected, so that it is possible to make changes in the list of variables or the data collection tools. When making a plan for data processing and analysis, the following steps should be included.

   i. Sorting data,

   ii. Performing quality-control checks, and

   iii. Processing data.

SORTING DATA

Sorting the data is important for subsequent processing and analysis. If one has different study populations, the questionnaires should be numbered separately.

- In a comparative study, it is best to sort the data into 2 or 3 groups that will be compared during data analysis.

- In a cross-section survey, it may be useful to sort the data into two or more groups depending on the objectives of the study.

PERFORMING QUALITY-CONTROL CHECKS

Before and during data processing, the information collected should be checked again for completeness and internal consistency.

PROCESSING DATA

A decision should be taken whether to process and analyse the data either manually by using data master sheets or by computer using software for analysis.

Data processing involves editing, categorizing, coding and tabulation.

Editing

Editing is the process of examining the data collected through questionnaires to detect errors and omissions and to see if they are ready for tabulation. The data collected should be as accurate as possible, consistent, uniformly entered, complete and acceptable for coding and tabulation.

Categorizing

First, it should be decided which of the data are quantitative and which are qualitative. Quantitative data are expressed in numbers that are presented in frequencies. When analysing the quantitative data, we should consider the objective/ purpose of the study. Some examples are listed below.

- Descriptive variables, e.g. distribution of teenage pregnancies in villages.
- Differences between the two groups, e.g. above poverty line and below poverty line.
- Association between variables, e.g. training and work efficiency.

For numerical data, the data are usually collected without any pre-categorization. Decisions concerning how to categorize numerical data are usually made after they have been collected.

Coding

Coding is a method used to convert the data gathered into symbols appropriate for analysis. While coding, much of the information in the raw data may be eliminated. So the researcher should carefully design category sets in order to utilize the available data more fully.

In the case of pre-coded questions, coding begins during the preparation of interview schedules. Then the coding frame is developed by listing the possible answer to each question and by assigning code numbers. The coding frame shows what is coded and how it is coded. Coded data can be entered in the transcription sheet either by hand or by using a computer.

If the data are to be processed by hand, it is necessary to summarize the raw data in a data master sheet where all the answers of the respondents are tallied by hand. Data are easier to tally from the master sheet than from orginal questionnaires. Questionnaire data may be compiled by hand instead of using master sheets if it is difficult or impossible to put the information in a master sheet. Hand compilation is used when the sample is small. Larger the sample, the more beneficial it is to use a computer.

Computer compilation consists of the following steps.

- Choosing an appropriate computer program
- Data entry
- Verification
- Programming
- Computer output

Choosing an appropriate computer program The most widely used programs are LOTUS 1-2-3, (a spreadsheet program), BASE and SPSS program.

Data entry One has to develop a data entry format depending on the program. Then the information on the data collection instrument needs to be coded, e.g. Male 1 and Female 2.

Verification Since the computer will print out the data exactly as it has been entered, the print out should be checked visually.

Programming If one uses computer personnel to analyse the data, it is important to communicate effectively with them. We should give

- a list of all the variables,
- the data format,
- subjects to be analysed and groups to be compared, and
- variables with straight tabulations and cross tabulations.

Computer output The computer can do all kinds of analysis. But we should choose the appropriate statistical tools to present the data as tables, graphs, and so on.

Summarizing

Tabulation is the process of summarizing raw data and displaying it in compact form for further analysis. It can be done by hand or by using a computer. Analysis of data is made possible only through tables.

14
DATA ANALYSIS

INTRODUCTION

The term analysis refers to the computation of certain statistical measures or indices such as average, standard deviation, correlation coefficient, etc. The purpose of analysis is to summarize and organize the collected data with a view to solve a variety of social, economic, and development problems; to help the investigator to bring new ideas and creative thinking into research investigations; and to draw conclusions and make suggestions for future courses of action. Analysis in the case of survey or experimental data includes estimating the population parameters and drawing inferences based on statistical tests. Thus, analysis of data is therefore broadly categorized into descriptive analysis and inferential analysis. A basic and proper understanding of these topics is very essential for carrying out proper data analysis in respect of the research problem under investigation.

DESCRIPTION OF VARIABLES

A variable is a characteristic which varies in magnitude or measurement, e.g. age of persons, number of children in different families, height, weight, income, expenditure, etc. The variables selected may be used to describe the problem (dependent variables) or they may be treated as contributory factors (independent variable) to the problem under study. The objective of data analysis is to determine which variables best describe the problem and which variables contribute to the problem.

The first step in statistical analysis is to summarize the data on each variable in simple tables or in a single figure (for example, average income).

Generally, the variables are grouped under the following categories.

- Nominal
- Ordinal
- Interval
- Ratio level

The first two levels are concerned with categorical data and the other two levels are concerned with numerical data.

CATEGORICAL DATA

Categorical data includes nominal and ordinal level measurements. The nominal level data of the variables are classified into a number of categories as given in Table 14.1.

Table 14.1   Categories of nominal level characteristics

Nominal characteristics	Categories
Residence	Rural, urban
Marital status	Single, married, widowed, separated and divorced

The variables under ordinal level measurements are divided into a number of categories, but ordered from the lowest to the highest (Table 14.2).

Table 14.2 Categories of ordinal level characteristics

Ordinal characteristics	Categories
Level of participation	Good, average, poor
Opinion on a statement	Fully agree, agree, no idea, disagree, highly disagree

NUMERICAL DATA

It refers to numerical measurements of a variable expressed in numbers. Numerical variables are of two types viz, discrete and continuous. A continuous variable is capable of manifesting every conceivable fractional value within the range of possibilities, e.g. the height of persons, the weight of a group of individuals.

On the other hand, a discrete variable is that which can vary only by finite 'jumps' and cannot manifest every conceivable fractional value, e.g. number of rooms in different houses, number of employees in different organizations, number of machines in different establishments.

An understanding of the nature of data and the type of variable determines the type of statistical measures to be used. Categorical data and numerical data can be examined in the following ways.

   i. Frequency distributions

   ii. Percentages, proportions, ratios and rates

   iii. Diagrams and graphs

Frequency Distribution

It refers to the data classified on the basis of some variables (discrete or continuous) that can be measured or classified.

Such variables include age, income, expenditure, number of children, price, wage, number of units produced or consumed.

Discrete variables   Variables with no possible values between adjacent units on the scale. It takes only integral values and not fractional values, e.g., family size, number of units produced, number of units consumed, etc.

Continuous variables   Variables that can have infinite number of values between adjacent units on the scale. It can take both integral and decimal values.

Accordingly, a frequency distribution can be discrete or continuous as given in Table 14.3.

Table 14.3   Frequency distributions

Discrete frequency distribution		Continuous frequency distribution	
No. of Children	No. of families	Weight (in lbs)	No. of persons
0	5	100–110	5
1	10	110–120	10
2	15	120–130	15
3	10	130–140	10
4	5	140–150	5
5	2	150–160	5
Total	47	Total	50

Frequency distributions in the case of categorical data (nominal and ordinal categories) may have a very few categories. A few illustrations are given below.

Nominal characteristic   This is based on nominal level measurements.

Example

The blood samples of 50 girls examined for malarial parasites are given in the form of a frequency distribution.

Table 14.4 Distribution of patients by malaria parasites

Parasite	No. of patients
Negative(no parasite)	25
P. falciparum	20
P. vivax	5
Total	50

From the above distribution, it is clear that 25 girls with a clinical diagnosis do not have malaria. Among the rest, *P. falciparum* (20 cases) is very much prevalent than *P. vivax* (5 cases).

Ordinal characteristic This is based on ordinal level measurements. An example is given below.

Example

A survey was conducted among health personnel from 170 rural health subcentres in Tamil Nadu.They were asked about the shortage of drugs for the treatment of malaria in the last 5 years. The following information was obtained.

Table 14.5 Distribution of subcentres by category order

Category order	Number of subcentres
No shortage of drugs	71
Rarely (1 to 5 times)	65
Occasionally (5 to 10 times)	20
Frequently (more than 10 times)	14
Total	170

The above is an example for a frequency distribution of an ordinal characteristic. The order indicates the severity of the problem about the shortage of drugs in the subcentres.

From the above frequency distribution, we see that most of the clinics either did not or rarely experienced shortage of antimalarial drugs. Further, it was an occasional problem in 20 cases and a severe problem in 14 cases.

Thus, the steps involved in making a frequency distribution of numerical measurements are the following.

- ✎ Decide the different groups.
- ✎ Count the number of observations in each group.

Note

The following points are to be kept in mind while preparing a frequency distribution of a numerical characteristic.

- ✎ The groups should not overlap.
- ✎ There must be continuity from one group to the other.
- ✎ The groups must be arranged from the lowest to the highest measurement.

Percentages, Proportions, Ratios and Rates

Percentages   Percentages are also called relative frequencies. They standardize the data, which facilitate comparison. A percentage is defined as the number of units possessing a particular characteristic divided by the total number of units in the whole group and multiplied by 100. It is given by

$$\% f_i = (f_i/n) \times 100$$

where, f_i is the class frequency.

In a frequency distribution table, the sum of all the percentages should be equal to 100.

A survey on daily income of 560 persons was carried out in an urban locality and the data are presented in Table 14.6.

Table 14.6 Percentage distribution of persons by daily income

Daily income (in Rs.)	No. of persons	Percentage
100–200	50	8.9
200–300	100	17.9
300–400	200	35.7
400–500	150	26.8
500–600	40	7.1
600–700	20	3.6
Total	560	100.0

Proportions A proportion is a value that compares one part of a group to the whole. It can be expressed as a fraction. The sum of all fractions in a frequency distribution should be equal to 1.00. It is given by

$$P_i = f_i/n$$

where,

f_i = frequency in the ith category, and

n = sample size.

Example

Suppose, in a company there are 500 workers, out of which 150 are females. Find the proportion of males and females employed by the company and comment on it.

Total number of workers   = 500

Number of female workers   = 150

Number of male workers	=	350
Proportion of female workers	=	150/500 = 0.3
Proportion of male workers	=	350/500 = 0.7
Total proportion	=	Proportion of male workers + Proportion of female workers
	=	0.7 + 0.3 = 1.0

The proportion of male workers is higher in the company.

Ratios   A ratio evaluates the size of one subclass relative to another subclass. In the case of a frequency distribution table, ratios can be used for comparing two different categories. It is represented by

$$\text{Ratio} = f_1/f_2 \text{ or } f_1:f_2$$

where,

f_1 = frequency in one class, and
f_2 = frequency in another class.

Examples

1. In a company, there are 600 male workers and 400 female workers. Find the ratio of female workers to male workers and comment on it.

   Ratio of females to males = Number of females/Number of males
   $$= 400/600 = 0.667.$$

   The ratio of females to males is 0.67. Therefore, there are 0.67 females per male in the company.

2. A survey was conducted in a village covering a sample of 504 males and 718 females. The following questions were asked in the survey.

   i. What is the ratio of males to females?

ii. What is the percentage of male members in the village?

iii. What is the percentage of females in the village?

The answers to these questions will be as follows:

Total number of respondents = 504 + 718 = 1222

Ratio of males to females = 504/718 = 0.70

Therefore, on an average, there are 0.70 males for every female in the village.

Percentage of males = (504/1222) × 100
= 41.24%

This implies that there are about 41% males in the village.

Percentage of females in the village = (718/1222) × 100
= 58.76%

That is, there are 59% females in the village.

Further, we can say that the village is dominated by females.

Rates A rate is the measure of a characteristic which is measured in a specified period of time. A rate is expressed per 1000 units. Certain commonly used rates are birth rate, death rate, infant mortality rate, couple protection rate and maternal mortality rate. Formulae for computation of these rates are given below.

$$\text{Birth rate (BR)} = \frac{\text{Number of live births}}{\text{Total population}} \times 1000$$

= the number of live births per 1000 population in a particular year

$$\text{Death rate (DR)} = \frac{\text{Number of deaths}}{\text{Total population}} \times 1000$$

= the number of deaths per 1000 population in a particular year

$$\text{Infant mortality rate (IMR)} = \frac{\text{Number of infant deaths below the age of one year}}{\text{Total number of live births}} \times 1000$$

= the number of infant deaths of less than one year per 1000 live births

$$\text{Maternal mortality rate (MMR)} = \frac{\text{Number of pregancy-related deaths in one year}}{\text{Total number of live births}} \times 1,00,000$$

= the number of pregnancy-related deaths in one year per 1,00,000 live births in the same year

$$\text{Couple protection rate (CPR)} = \frac{\text{Number of eligible women}}{\text{Total number of users of different methods of FP}} \times 1000$$

= the number of FP users of all methods per 1000 eligible women

Diagrams and Graphs

Classification and tabulation in the form of different frequency distributions discussed as earlier, help us to summarize and present the data in a systematic manner. The data can also be presented through diagrams and graphs. Such diagrams and graphs are often found in newspapers, journals, advertisements, etc. Data presented through diagrams and graphs are always convincing and very appealing to the human mind and last for a long time. Further, it facilitates comparison among different groups.

Merits

✎ The information presented through diagrams and graphs are easily understood.

✎ They are attractive to the eyes.

✎ They are very popular in exhibitions, fairs, conferences, etc.

✎ They are easy to remember.

✎ They facilitate comparison of data, viz., over a period of time or at a point of time between two places.

The frequently used diagrams and graphs in data analysis are the following.

✎ Bar diagrams

✎ Pie diagram

✎ Histogram

✎ Line graph

✎ Scatter diagram

Bar diagram It is a type of diagrammatic presentation of data in which bars are drawn to represent the distribution of cases. The bars represent proportionately the quantities being compared. This is especially used to describe the distribution of a qualitative variable (non-measurable characteristic).

Example

A survey was conducted among health personnel from 200 rural health subcentres in Tamil Nadu. They were asked: How often were you short of drugs for the treatment of malaria in the last five years? The following is the distribution obtained.

Shortage of drugs	Number of subcentres	Percentage
Never	71	35.5
Rarely (1 to 5 times)	65	32.5
Occasionally (5 to 10 times)	40	20.0
Frequently (10+)	24	12.0
Total	200	100.0

Represent the above data by a simple bar diagram.

Diagram 1   Bar diagram using frequencies

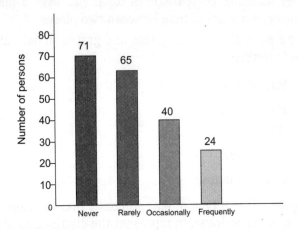

Shortage of anti-malarial drugs in 200 rural health subcentres in Tamil Nadu

Diagram 2   Bar diagram using percentages

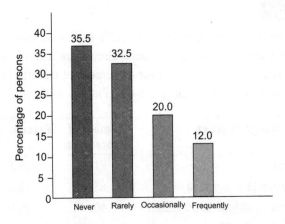

Shortage of anti-malarial drugs in 200 rural health subcentres in Tamil Nadu

Note that the widths of the bars in the above diagrams are the same; only the height varies. Also, the space between each bar remains the same.

Pie diagram A pie diagram is used to show percentage breakdowns or relative frequency of different items. It is so called because the entire diagram looks like a pie. The components resemble slices cut from a pie. The total percentage of all the items should be equal to 100.

Example

The problem given in the previous example can also be illustrated in the form of a pie diagram as shown below:

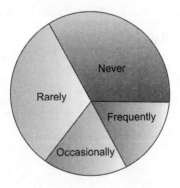

Pie diagram representing shortage of anti-malarial drugs in 200 rural health subcentres in Tamil Nadu

Histogram Frequency distributions of numerical data are often presented in the form of histograms. This is very popular and widely used in practice. It is defined as a set of vertical bars in which the areas are proportionate to the frequencies. While drawing histograms, the characteristic is taken along the x-axis and the corresponding frequencies along the y-axis. An illustration is given below.

Example

One hundred rural health subcentres in a district in Tamil Nadu were asked to submit a report on the number of patients treated for anaemia in the last one year ending 31st March 2008. The data are given below in the form of a frequency distribution. Draw a histogram.

Number of patients treated	Number of health centres
0–19	30
20–39	5
40–59	7
60–79	14
80–99	22
100–119	12
120–139	6
140–159	4
Total	100

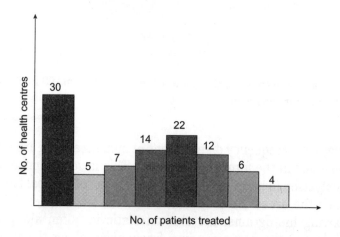

Histogram of no. of patients treated for anaemia in 100 rural health subcentres

Line graph A line graph is generally used for presenting time series data, i.e., data recorded over a period of time. It shows the trend over time. One can show two or more frequency distributions at a time in the form of line graphs. Through comparison, data trends can be visualized. A line graph is illustrated below.

Example

Below are given the number of malarial cases treated by health centres in a district. Present the data in the form of a line graph.

Day	Cases	Day	Cases	Day	Cases
1	9	8	16	15	28
2	12	9	16	16	28
3	11	10	18	17	28
4	13	11	19	18	32
5	14	12	16	19	21
6	13	13	21	20	19
7	16	14	25	21	12
Total	88	Total	131	Total	168

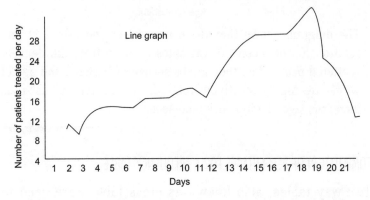

Line graph showing number of cases treated by health centres in a district

Scatter diagram A dot chart or spread of points on a graph sheet is called a scatter diagram. It is used for presenting data on two related variables. This is the first step in the analysis of relationship between two variables, especially correlation. A scatter diagram is illustrated below with an example.

Example

Present the following data in the form of a scatter diagram.

Age of husbands (yrs): 22 25 26 28 30 32 34 37 41 45

Age of wives (yrs): 18 20 21 25 26 29 32 35 40 41

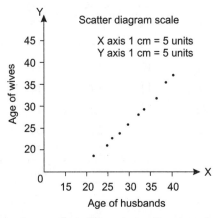

The diagram shows that there is a direct and also a strong relationship between the variables as seen from the densely scattered points, i.e., the variables—age of husband and age of wife—are highly positively related, i.e., as age of husbands increases, age of wives also increases.

COMPUTATION OF PERCENTAGES FOR A FREQUENCY TABLE

Two-way tables, also known as cross tables, are used to condense and present the data. Through such tables, it is also possible to determine if two variables are related or not.

Because of varying row and column totals, it is very difficult to detect the effect of an independent variable on a dependent variable. However, one can calculate the percentages and can compare the cell frequencies. A frequency table can be percentaged in the following ways.

    i. Percentages by total or total percentages

   ii. Percentages by column total or column percentages

  iii. Percentages by row total or row percentages

Let us briefly explain these with illustrations and see how comparison is made.

Total Percentages (Percentages by Total)

These percentages are worked out on the basis of the grand total. This procedure is followed when we are not able to distinguish between independent and dependent variables included in the analysis.

Example

From the following table showing the distribution of political parties by sex, compute total percentages.

Political party favoured	No. of males	%	No. of females	%	Total No.	Total %
DPA	43	21.5	17	8.5	60	30
UPA	77	38.5	63	31.5	140	70
Total	120	60	80	40	200	100

The percentages in the above table are interpreted in relation to the total number of cases in the table. The sum of all the percentages in the cells equals 100, and the column or the row total equals 100.

Column Percentages (Percentages by Column Total)

The column percentages are calculated when the independent variable is placed at the top as column heading. The sum of all these percentages, will add to 100 in each column. In the case of column percentages, comparison will be made in each row. If all the percentages are similar in each row of the table, a weak or no association is observed. On the other hand, if the percentages are different in each row, we can say that there is an association between the variables under investigation. An illustration of column percentages for the above example is given below.

Table 14.7   Computation of column percentages

Political party	Gender (%)		Total
	Male	Female	
DPA	35.8	21.3	30
UPA	64.2	78.7	70
Total	100.0	100.0	100

The percentages in Table 14.7 are interpreted in relation to the column total.

Row Percentages (Percentages by Row Total)

If the independent variable is placed on the left side as a row heading, row per cents shall be calculated. The sum of all these percentages will add to 100 in each row. When row percentages are calculated, comparison will be made in each column. If all the percentages are similar in each column, a weak or no association is inferred and vice versa. The table below shows the computation of row percentages.

Table 14.8 Computation of row percentages

Political party	Gender (%)		Total
	Male	Female	
DPA	71.7	28.3	100
UPA	55.0	45.0	100
Total	60.0	40.0	100

These percentages are interpreted in relation to the total number of cases in each row (Table 14.8).

CROSS TABULATION

So far we have dealt with observations collected on a single variable. These are used to describe the variable partially. However, there are situations wherein we may be interested in examining the relationship between two or more variables to identify possible explanations for it. To achieve this, we may have to resort to cross tabulations.

TYPES OF CROSS TABULATIONS

Depending on the objectives of the study, the following cross tabulations are suggested.

  i. Cross tabulations that describe a sample.
 ii. Cross tabulations in which groups are compared to determine differences, if any.
iii. Cross tabulations that focus on exploring relationships between variables.

Below are given illustrative examples to deal with these types of cross tabulations.

Cross tabulations to describe a sample A study was conducted to find the degree of job satisfaction among doctors and nurses in rural and urban areas. In order to describe the sample, a cross table was prepared and presented as given in Table 14.9.

Table 14.9   Distribution of doctors and nurses by residence and sex

Health personnel	Residence		Total
	Rural (%)	Urban (%)	
Doctors			
Males	8 (10)	35 (21)	43
Females	2 (3)	16 (10)	18
Nurses			
Males	46 (58)	36 (22)	82
Females	23 (29)	77 (47)	100
Total	79 (100)	164 (100)	243

The above table is useful because the opinions of male and female staff are compared separately for rural and urban areas. It contains absolute values (or frequencies) and the corresponding percentages (or relative frequencies). It is also possible to have either the mean, median and/or modal value if the data is numerical in character. In descriptive studies that aim at quantification of certain characteristics, cross tabulation is a highly useful tool for presenting the findings.

Cross tabulations to determine differences between groups   In some studies, we may be interested to know whether there is any difference between two or more groups on a particular characteristic. This is the case in respect of certain studies such as case–control studies, Cohort studies or quasi-experimental studies. In such cases, cross tabulation of data is necessary. Cross tabulation is depicted in the following example.

Example

In an experimental study on the effect of attendance of mothers at nutrition talks on their level of nutritional knowledge, two groups of mothers were compared: those who attended and those who did not attended the nutrition talks. The following dummy table (Table 14.10) was prepared.

Table 14.10 Attendance of mothers at nutrition talks vs different levels of nutritional knowledge

Characteristic of mothers	Level of nutritional knowledge			Total
	Low	Average	High	
Attended				
Not attended				
Total				

In the above table, level of nutritional knowledge is the dependent variable and is the outcome of the attendance at nutrition talks. Attendance is therefore the independent variable. In general, in a cross tabulation analysis, the dependent variables are kept in columns and the independent variables in rows.

Cross tabulations to analyse relationship between variables   In order to determine whether two variables are associated or not, we should find which are the independent variables and which are the dependent variables. For example, while analysing the relationship between age of mother and duration of breast-feeding (Table 14.11), or duration of breast-feeding and work status of mother (Table 14.12), the cross tabulations will have the following forms.

Table 14.11 Duration of breast-feeding vs age groups of mothers

Age (years)	Duration of breast feeding			Total
	0–6 months	6–12 months	12+ months	
15–19				
20–24				
25–29				
30–34				
35–39				
Total				

Table 14.12 Duration of breast-feeding vs work status of mothers

Work status of mothers	Duration of breast feeding			Total
	0–6 months	6–12 months	12+ months	
Full-time employed				
Part-time employed				
Unemployed				
Total				

For the above tables, we can use correlation or association measures to determine the relationship between the variables/attributes (non-measurable characteristic).

STATISTICAL MEASURES

The important statistical measures used to summarize the data are the following.

    i. Central measures (mean, median and mode),

   ii. Dispersion measures (range and standard deviation),

  iii. Measures of skewness and kurtosis,

iv. Correlation and association measures, and

v. Other measures.

Amongst the central measures, mean, median and mode are frequently used. They are used to represent the group characteristics. Also they facilitate comparison.

Dispersion measures are also known as variability measures. They include range, quartile deviation (QD), mean deviation (MD), standard deviation (SD) and coefficient of variation (CV). Of these measures, range, SD and CV are frequently used to judge the reliability of the central measures and also for judging the consistency of the observations.

Measures of skewness are based on mean and mode or mean and median. They are used to analyse the symmetry of the data. Measures of kurtosis are used to understand the peakness or flatness of the distribution.

Correlation/association measures are used to assess the nature and the strength of the relationship between variables. Regression analysis is used to estimate the unknown values of a variable from the known values of the other related variable.

Multiple correlation, partial correlation, multiple regression and partial regression are the other important measures used in data analysis.

Let us briefly discuss these measures in the following pages, with illustrations.

CENTRAL MEASURES

An important objective of statistical analysis is to get one single value in order to represent the entire mass of unwieldy data. Such a value is called an average or the central value or a central measure or a measure of central tendency. An average is a measure that represents a set of values. It depicts the characteristic of the entire group.

The objectives of a central measure are

- ✎ to get one single value that describes the characteristic of the entire group.
- ✎ to facilitate comparison.

Most commonly used central measures are the mean, the median and the mode. Other measures such as geometric mean, harmonic mean, progressive average and moving average are also used, but rarely.

Mean

Mean is also called as arithmetic mean/average/arithmetic average. It is defined as the sum of all the values divided by the total number of values. It is denoted by $\bar{X}$ and is given by

$$\bar{X} = \frac{\Sigma X}{n}$$

where,

X = Value of the variable and

n = Number of values.

Mean is generally used in the case of interval and ratio level measurements.

Example

The following are the heights of 10 women as obtained through a survey. Compute the mean height.

Height (cm): 142, 143, 141, 143, 144, 145, 155, 146, 148, 147.

$$\text{Mean} = \frac{\Sigma X}{n}$$

where,

X = Height measurements and

n = No. of women

Here,

$$\Sigma X = 142 + 143 + \dots + 147 = 1454$$
$$n = 10$$

∴ Mean = 1454/10 = 145.4 cm.

Therefore, the average height of women is 145.4 cm. Further, there are 6 women whose height is below the average height observed.

Median

Median is also called positional average. It divides the distribution into two equal parts. The number of observations below the median value is equal to the number of observations above the median value. It is defined as the middle value in the series of data arranged in ascending or descending order of magnitude. It is denoted by the symbol M_d and is given by

M_d = size of $\left(\dfrac{n+1}{2}\right)^{th}$ value in the series arranged in ascending or descending order of magnitude.

Here, n is the number of observations given. If n is even, then the value of median is the average of the middle two items in the arranged series. Median is used mostly in the case of ordinal level measurements.

Example

Calculate the median income from the following observations.

Monthly income Rs. : 280, 190, 96, 98, 104, 75, 80, 94, 100, 75, 500, 180

Calculation

Median = Size of the middle value in the arranged series
= size of 6.5th value in the arranged series

Arranged series: 75, 75, 80, 94, 96, 98, 100, 104, 180, 190, 280, 500

Median = (98 + 100)/2 = Rs. 99 (since the number of observations are even.)

Mode

Mode is also called the most typical or fashionable value of a distribution. It occurs frequently in a distribution. It is defined as the most frequently occurring value in a given set of values. It is denoted by the symbol Mo. Thus, mode is the most frequently occurring value or the value that has got the highest number of occurrences over other values. It is often used as a central measure in the case of categorical data, viz., nominal or ordinal level measurements.

Example

Below are given the data on family size surveyed in a village. Calculate the modal family size in the village.

Family size: 3, 0, 1, 2, 2, 1, 2, 3, 2, 2, 0, 4, 2, 2, 0, 2, 2, 2, 5, 2, 2, 6.

Calculation

By definition, mode = the most frequently occurring value.

Among the values given, 2 has occurred 12 times whereas other values have occurred with very less frequency.

Hence , Mo = 2.

Modal family size is 2 children. That is, most of the families in the village have got two children. This implies that the families are adhering to small family norm.

Note

Mean is frequently used because it is based on all the values. However, it is affected very much by extreme observations, while the median and the mode are not. The calculation of mean and its understanding is the basis for higher level statistical analysis.

The selection of an average depends on the following considerations:

- The level of measurement of data.
- The shape of the frequency distribution.
- The purpose of calculating the measure.

Further, if the variable is nominal, mode is the best choice.

- If the variable is ordinal, both median and mode can be used.
- If the distribution is normal (symmetrical or bell-shaped), all the three measures will have the same value and hence any one of the measures can be used.
- In the case of a skewed distribution (different from normal distribution), median is a better measure of central tendency than mean or mode.

Relationship Among the Averages

1. If mean = median = mode, the distribution is symmetrical or normal.
2. If mean > median > mode, the distribution is positively skewed.
3. If mean < median < mode, the distribution is negatively skewed.

Example

The following table gives the daily income of 12 families in a village.

Daily income (Rs.): 280, 180, 96, 98, 104, 75, 80, 94, 100, 75, 600, 200
Calculate the mean, median and modal incomes. Which average would represent the series best? Why?

Calculation of Mean

$$\text{Mean} = \frac{\Sigma X}{n}$$

where,

X = daily income and

n = number of families

Therefore, mean income = $\dfrac{1982}{12}$ = Rs. 165.17

That is, the average income of the families is Rs. 165.17

Calculation of Median

By definition, Median = size of $\left(\dfrac{n+1}{2}\right)^{th}$ observation in the series arranged in ascending or descending order of magnitude.

Arranged observations: 75, 75, 80, 94, 96, 98, 100, 104, 180, 200, 280, 600.

Here

$$\frac{n+1}{2} = \frac{12+1}{2} = 6.5\text{th value in the above series}$$

∴ Median income = (98 + 100)/2
$$= \text{Rs. } 99$$

That is, the median income of the families is Rs. 99.

Calculation of Mode

By definition, mode is the most frequently occurring value.

Here, 75 has occurred twice.

Hence, Mo = Rs. 75

Therefore, the modal income of the families is Rs. 75.

Inference

Here, median represents the series best, because there are more number of values around the median value.

ᕅᕆᕅᕆᕅᕆᕅᕆᕅᕆᕅ

Correcting an Incorrect Average

When an error is committed in the calculation of mean, it can be rectified. The process is very simple and is illustrated below with an example.

Example

The average score obtained by 50 boys in a class was 44. Later on, it was discovered that a score of 36 was misread as 56. Find the correct average score corresponding to the correct score.

Solution

Given: n = 50, $\overline{X} = 44$

We know that,

$$\overline{X} = \frac{\Sigma X}{n}$$
$$\Sigma X = n\overline{X}$$
$$= 50 \times 44$$
$$\text{wrong total} = 2200$$

$$\text{Correct total} = (2200 - 56) + 36$$
$$= 2180$$

$$\therefore \text{Correct average} = \frac{\text{Correct total}}{\text{Number of boys}}$$
$$= \frac{2180}{50}$$
$$= 43.6$$

Hence, the correct average is 43.6 scores.

❁❁❁❁❁❁❁

Combined average   If we have two or more similar groups to be merged together to get a single average, the process is very simple. This is done by calculating the combined average. The combined average is denoted by $\bar{X}$ given by

$$\bar{\bar{X}} = \frac{n_1 \bar{X}_1 + n_2 \bar{X}_2}{n_1 + n_2}$$

n_1 = No. of observations in the first group,

$\bar{X}_1$ = Average of the first group,

n_2 = No. of observations in the second group and

$\bar{X}_2$ = Average of the second group.

Examples

1. The mean height of 25 workers in Factory A is 61 cm and the mean height of 35 workers in Factory B is 58 cm. Find the combined mean height of all the workers in factories A and B taken together.

Solution

$$\bar{X} = \frac{n_1 \bar{X}_1 + n_2 \bar{X}_2}{n_1 + n_2}$$

Here,

$$n_1 = 25, \ \bar{X}_1 = 61$$
$$n_2 = 35, \ \bar{X}_2 = 58$$

Therefore,

$$\bar{\bar{X}} = \frac{(25 \times 61) + (35 \times 58)}{25 + 35}$$
$$= \frac{1525 + 2030}{60}$$
$$= \frac{3555}{60} = 59.25$$

Therefore, the combined mean height of all the 60 workers in the factories A and B taken together is 59.25 cm.

2. The following are the number of passengers carried on each of 50 journeys by an aircraft with a seating capacity of 100. Calculate the following.

   i. the average capacity used, and

   ii. if 65 passengers is the smallest profitable load, the proportion of flights which were unprofitable.

10	18	61	65	72	78	82	25	45	66	68	95	92
31	41	56	33	78	65	72	74	89	67	68	32	46
49	35	37	43	55	57	69	72	84	89	92	75	83
68	72	45	45	39	11	37	38	62	69	72		

i. **Calculation of average capacity used**

$$\text{Average capacity used} = \frac{\Sigma X}{n}$$

where,

   X = number of passengers and

   n = number of trips.

Here,

$$\Sigma X = 10 + 31 + 49 + 68 + 18 + \ldots + 46 + 83$$
$$= 2927$$
$$n = 50$$

Therefore,

$$\bar{X} = \frac{2927}{50} = 58.54$$

Thus, the average capacity used is 58.54 persons per trip.

Inference

The average capacity used reveals that the trips were unprofitable on the whole. However, there were good number of trips which were highly profitable.

ii. Calculation of proportion of unprofitable trips

The number of flights that carried passengers below 65 is 23. Hence,

Proportion of flights which were unprofitable $= \dfrac{23}{50} \times 100 = 46\%$

Inference

On the whole, 46% of the trips were unprofitable by the aircraft.

DISPERSION MEASURES

Mean, median and mode discussed earlier are used to describe the central part of the distribution. They are called the central values or the measures of central tendency. They do not give us any idea about the variation/dispersion in the measurements of a variable. Therefore, we need some measures of variability. They should describe the variation of the measurements with respect to some central value (mean or median or mode).

The objectives of dispersion measures are

- ✎ to determine the reliability of an average.
- ✎ to serve as a basis for the control of variability.
- ✎ to compare two or more series with regard to variability.
- ✎ to facilitate the use of other statistical measures such as correlation, regression, etc.

The different measures of dispersion are range, quartile deviation, mean deviation, and standard deviation. Of these, range and standard deviation are frequently used in data analysis. Therefore, a brief description of these measures and their associated measures are discussed here with suitable illustrations.

Range

Range is the simplest measure of variation. It is defined as the difference between the smallest and the largest values in a given set of values. It is denoted by R and is given by

$$R = L - S$$

where,

L = largest value, and

S = the smallest value.

This is an absolute measure of variation and is expressed in the same unit of measurement. The relative measure of range (R) is known as coefficient of range (CR) and is given by

$$CR = \frac{L - S}{L + S}$$

This is free from the unit of measurement and facilitates easy comparison between two or more groups.

Example

The weights of a group of pregnant mothers in a village are given below.

Weight: 43, 44, 42, 52, 56, 62, 40, 41, 47 kg.

Calculate range and its coefficient.

Calculation

Range (R) = L – S

Here, L = 62, and S = 40

Therefore, R = 62 – 40 = 22 kg

Coefficient of range, (CR) = (62 – 40/62 + 40) = 22/102 = 0.22

Range, as a measure of variation, is used to compare two or more comparable series with regard to variability. The group that has a lesser range value is said to be more homogeneous than the group with a higher range value. In the same way, coefficient of range is used for comparing variation between two or more groups. Range is not a good measure of dispersion, because it is based on the two extreme values which are subject to fluctuations of sampling.

Standard Deviation

This is regarded as the best measure of variation, in the sense that it satisfies almost all the characteristics for a good measure of variation. It is defined as the positive square root of the means of the squared deviations from the mean. It is used to describe how much individual measurements differ on the average from the mean. It is denoted by σ and is given by

$$\sigma = \sqrt{\Sigma(X - \bar{X})^2 / n}$$

when deviations are taken from mean, and

$$\sigma = \sqrt{\Sigma(d^2 / n) - (\Sigma d / n)^2} \quad (d = X - A)$$

when the deviations are taken from assumed mean.

Combined standard deviation Like combined mean, we can also calculate combined SD. The formula for combined SD is given by

$$\sigma_{1,2} = \sqrt{\frac{n_1(\sigma_1^2 + d_1^2) + n_2(\sigma_2^2 + d_2^2)}{n_1 + n_2}}$$

where, n_1, $\bar{X}_1, \sigma_1$ and n_2, $\bar{X}_2, \sigma_2$ are the sample size, average and SD of the two samples respectively.

Here $d_1 = \bar{\bar{X}} - \bar{X}_1$

$d_2 = \bar{\bar{X}} - \bar{X}_2$

Example

From the observations given below, compute SD.

Weight (kg) : 43, 60, 48, 37, 48, 65, 57, 78, 59, 31

Calculation (by assumed mean method)

X	$d = X - 50$	d^2
43	−7	49
60	10	100
48	−2	4
37	−13	169
48	−2	4
65	15	225
57	7	49
78	28	784
59	9	81
31	−19	361
Total	26	1826

Here $A = 50$

$$\Sigma d = 26, \Sigma d^2 = 1826$$

$$\sigma = \sqrt{\frac{\Sigma d^2}{n} - \left(\frac{\Sigma d}{n}\right)^2}$$

$$= \sqrt{1826/10 - (26 - 10)^2}$$

$$= \sqrt{182.6 - 6.76}$$

$$= \sqrt{175.84}$$

$$= 13.26 \text{ units}$$

$$\therefore \ SD = 13.26 \text{ units}$$

SD-based measures   CSD and CV are the two SD based measures. Coefficient of SD (CSD) is always a fraction and free from unit of measurement. Coefficient of variation (CV) is always expressed in percentage.

$$\text{Coefficient of SD (CSD)} = \sigma / \bar{X}$$

$$\text{Coefficient of variation (CV)} = (\sigma / \bar{X}) \times 100$$

How to use CSD or CV   The measure CSD or CV is used for the purpose of comparing variability of observations between two or more groups. Higher the variation, greater will be the value of CV and vice versa. Higher the value of CV, lesser the homogeniety of the observations, or less consistent. In such cases, the average is less reliable.

Example

Below are given the performance scores of two students in 10 tests (out of 100 marks each).

Test	1	2	3	4	5	6	7	8	9	10
Student X	25	50	45	30	70	42	36	48	34	60
Student Y	10	70	50	20	95	55	42	60	48	80

Further, their average scores, SD and CV are given below.

Measures	Student X	Student Y
Average (marks)	44	53
SD (marks)	13.08	24.35
CV (%)	29.72	45.94

Draw your inference.

Inference

Student Y is regarded as more intelligent, because his average score is more than the average score of X. However, student X is regarded as more consistent because his overall variation in the performance is only 29.72% compared to 45.94% variation in the scores obtained by Y. Hence, student Y is more intelligent and student X is more consistent.

❦❦❦❦❦❦❦❦

Steps to be followed in the calculation of standard deviation

1. Calculate the mean of all the values given.
2. Get the difference between the individual values and the mean.
3. Square all these differences.
4. Get the sum of all the squared differences obtained in step 3.
5. Divide this sum by n (in the case of large sample) and by $n-1$ (in the case of small sample).
6. Finally take the square root of the value obtained in step 5.

Note

A large standard deviation shows higher variability of values around the mean, while a small standard deviation shows lesser variability/dispersion of values around the mean.

Example

An analysis of the daily wages paid to workers in two firms A and B belonging to the same industry gives the following results.

Characteristic	Firm A	Firm B
Number of workers	550	650
Average daily wages (Rs.)	50	45
SD of the wages	$\sqrt{90}$	$\sqrt{120}$

Answer the following questions with proper justifications.

1. Which firm (A or B) pays out larger amount as daily wages?

2. In which firm (A or B) is there greater variability in individual wages?

3. Calculate the following.

   i. average monthly wages, and

   ii. SD of individual wages of all workers in the two firms taken together.

Solution

1. To answer which firm pays out larger amount as daily wages, compute and compare the total wage bills of the firms A and B separately.

   Total wage bill for A = 550 × 50 = Rs. 27,500

   Total wage bill for B = 650 × 45 = Rs. 29,250

From this, we conclude that firm B pays out larger amount as daily wages.

2. To answer which firm has greater variability in individual wages, we compute coefficient of variation (CV)

$$CV(A) = \frac{\sigma}{A} \times 100 = \frac{\sqrt{90}}{50} \times 100 = 18.97\%$$

$$CV(B) = \frac{\sigma}{\bar{B}} \times 100 = \frac{\sqrt{120}}{45} \times 100 = 24.34\%$$

From this, we conclude that the variability is more in the individual wages of workers in firm B.

3. To calculate combined mean $(\bar{\bar{X}})$ and combined standard deviation $(\sigma_{1,2})$:

Combined mean $(\bar{\bar{X}})$:

$$\bar{\bar{X}} = \frac{n_1 \bar{X}_1 + n_2 \bar{X}_2}{n_1 + n_2}$$

$$= \frac{(550 \times 50) + (650 \times 45)}{550 + 650}$$

$$= Rs.\,47.29$$

Combined standard deviation $(\sigma_{1,2})$:

$$\sigma_{1,2} = \sqrt{\frac{n_1 \sigma_1^2 + n_2 \sigma_2^2 + n_1 d_1^2 + n_2 d_2^2}{n_1 + n_2}}, \quad \begin{aligned} d_1 &= \bar{\bar{X}} - \bar{X}_1 \\ d_2 &= \bar{\bar{X}} - \bar{X}_2 \end{aligned}$$

$$= \sqrt{\frac{550 \times 90 + 650 \times 120 + 550 \times 7.34 + 650 \times 5.24}{550 + 650}}$$

$$= \sqrt{\frac{134943}{1200}}$$

$$= Rs.\,10.60$$

Results

1. Firm B pays out larger amount as daily wages.

2. There is greater variability in the individual wages of the workers in firm B.

3. i. The combined mean daily wage is Rs. 47.29.

   ii. The combined SD of daily wages of the two firms A and B taken together is Rs. 10.6.

NORMAL/SYMMETRICAL DISTRIBUTION

Many variables in social sciences follow a normal distribution. A normal distribution will have a bell-shaped curve with most of the values clustered around the mean and a few values away from the mean. The normal distribution is symmetrical about the mean. All the three measures of average will have the same value in the case of normal or symmetrical distribution, i.e., Mean = Median = Mode.

For a normal distribution, the following area relationships hold good.

i. Mean + 1σ covers 68.27% of the items in the distribution.

ii. Mean + 2σ covers 95.45% of the items in the distribution.

iii. Mean + 3σ covers 99.73% of the items in the distribution.

Example

Given below is an example for a symmetrical frequency distribution.

Value	Frequency
0–10	5
10–20	10
20–30	15
30–40	20
40–50	25
50–60	20
60–70	15
70–80	10
80–90	5
Total	125

The frequency curve of the above distribution illustrates the normal curve which is bell-shaped.

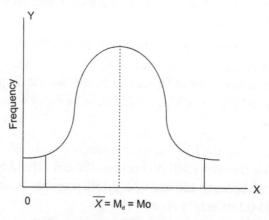

An important characteristic of a normally distributed variable is that 95% of the measurements will have values within 2 standard deviation (SD) of the mean. This is shown in the following figure.

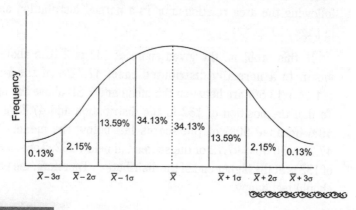

Examples

1. In a sample study, it was found that a group of 120 women had a mean height of 158 cm and a standard deviation of 3 cm. Normality of the variable implies that 95% of the women

were between 152 and 164 cm (assuming that the variable height is normally distributed). Further 2.5% of the women were shorter than 152 cm and 2.5% (or 3 women) were taller than 164 cms.

2. A population consists of 10,000 IQ scores. The distribution of IQ scores is normally distributed with an average of 100 and standard deviation of 16. If a particular student in the population has an IQ score of 132, would he/she be happy or sad?

Solution

It is given that the IQ scores are normally distributed. Therefore 34.13% of the scores will fall between 100 and 116; 13.59% of the scores fall between 116 and 132; 2.15% scores between 132 and 148; and 0.13% scores above 148.

Similarly 34.13% of the scores will fall between 84 and 100; 13.59% scores between 68 and 84; 2.15% scores between 52 and 68 and 0.13% scores below 52. These percentages are obtained by following the area relationships in a normal distribution shown in page 151.

In this problem, the given score of 132 is 2 SDs above the mean. In a normally distributed case, 47.72% of the scores (34.13 + 13.59) are between the mean and 2 SD above the mean. To find the position of 132 in the distribution add 47.72% with 50% because 50% of the scores fall below the mean. Thus, 47.72 + 50.00 = 97.72 of the scores fall below 132. Thus, a score of 132 is at the higher end of the distribution. Therefore, the person should feel happy.

POPULATION—SAMPLE RELATIONSHIP

The measures obtained based on a sample study are known as statistics which include mean, SD, etc. Such measures in the population are called parameters (μ, σ, etc.). The sample statistics can be used to describe the population characteristics. Further the sample statistics are used as estimates of population.

CONFIDENCE INTERVAL

It is an interval or a range of values which are most likely to include the population value. The lower and upper limits of this interval are called confidence limits. The calculation of confidence interval is based on a measure called standard error which is based on the standard deviation of the sample. The standard error of the mean is calculated by dividing the SD by the square root of the sample size, i.e., $SE_r = SD / \sqrt{n}$.

95% Confidence Interval of Mean

It implies that about 95% of all possible sample means lie within the population mean. In other words, we can say that we are about 95% sure that the population mean is within this interval.

Example

In a sample study, it is found that the mean weight of 15 four-year-old children is 17 kg with a SD of 3 kg. Obtain the confidence interval for the four-year-old children in the population.

Solution

Given: $n = 15$, $\bar{X} = 17\,\text{kg}$, $SD = 3$ kg.

$SE_r = 3 / \sqrt{15} = 3 / 3.873 = 0.775$.

Therefore, 95% confidence interval is $17 \pm 2 \times 0.775 = 15.5$ to 18.6.

Inference

We are approximately 95% sure that the mean weight of all four-year-old children in the population lies between 15.5 and 18.6 kg.

Note

The larger the sample size, the smaller the standard error and narrower the confidence interval. Thus the advantage of having a larger sample size is that the sample mean will be a better estimate of the population mean.

95% Confidence Interval of Percentage

The procedure for the calculation of confidence interval of a percentage is the same as the computation of confidence interval of a mean excepting that the data is categorical in the former case. This is illustrated below.

Example

A sample of 120 TB patients was drawn from a population of TB patients in the country. It was observed that 23.3% did not comply with their out-patient treatment. Others exhibited a satisfactory degree of compliance. Compute 95% confidence interval of the percentage of non-complier.

Calculation

Standard error of a percentage 'P' is given by

$$SE_r = \sqrt{P(100 - p)/n}$$

Here P = 23.3, 100 − P = 76.7.

∴ Standard error = $\sqrt{23.3 \times 76.7/120}$ = 3.9

95% confidence interval for the population percentage is 23.3% $\pm 2 \times 3.9$, i.e., 15.5% to 31.1%.

Inference

In the population of all TB patients in the country, 15.5% to 31.1% did not comply with their out-patient treatment.

CORRELATION AND REGRESSION ANALYSIS

The objective of regression and correlation analysis is to analyse the relationship between two variables in order to predict or estimate the value of one variable from the known value of the other variable.

CORRELATION ANALYSIS

If a change in one variable produces a change in the other variable, then we say that the variables are related or correlated.

Example

- Correlation between family income and weight of children.
- Correlation between income and expenditure of a group of people.
- Correlation between marriage age of girls and their achieved family size.

Types of Correlation

The following are the different types of correlation.

    i. Positive and negative correlation

   ii. Simple, partial and multiple correlation

  iii. Linear and non-linear correlation

Positive correlation If a change in one variable (X) produces a change in the other variable (Y) in the same direction, then correlation is said to be positive or the variables are said to be positively correlated.

Examples

X	1	2	3	4	5	6	7	8	9
Y	10	11	12	13	14	15	16	17	18

X1	16	17	18	19	20	21	22	23
Y2	20	22	23	24	24	25	26	26

Negative correlation If a change in one variable (X) produces a change in the other variable (Y) in the opposite direction, then the variables are said to be negatively correlated or inversely related.

Examples

X	51	54	56	59	65	60	70
Y	38	44	33	36	33	23	13

Price	11	12	13	14	15	16	17	18	19	20
Supply	30	29	29	25	24	24	24	21	18	15

Simple correlation A study of relationship between two variables only is known as simple correlation. It is denoted by the symbol $r_{1,2}$ or $r_{x,y}$, where, 1 and 2 or x and y represent variables under investigation.

Examples

- Correlation between income and expenditure
- Correlation between education and development
- Correlation between education and participation

Partial correlation A study of relationship between two variables while treating the other variable as constant is called partial correlation. It is denoted by $r_{1,2,3}$, $r_{1,3,2}$ or $r_{2,3,1}$ in the three-variables situation.

Multiple correlation A study of relationship between a variable and a set constituted by a number of variables is known as multiple correlation. It is denoted by the symbol $R_{1,2,3}$, $R_{2,1,3}$ and $R_{3,1,2}$ in three-variables situation.

Linear correlation Two variables are said to be linearly positively related if they both move together proportionately in the same direction and vice versa.

Example

X	1	2	3	4	5	6	7	8	9
Y	5	10	15	20	25	30	35	40	45

Non-linear correlation A correlation which is not linear is said to be a non-linear correlation. In the linear relationship, the points will fall on the line or will fall around the line. On the other hand, in the non-linear relationship, the points will fall on the curve or will fall around the curve as shown in Figure 14.1.

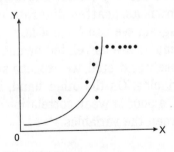

Figure 14.1 Scatter diagram showing non-linear relationship

Uses of Correlation Analysis

✎ With the help of correlation analysis, we can measure in one figure, the degree or strength of relationship as well as the nature of relationship.

✎ Correlation facilitates the estimation of one variable from the known value of another variable through regression analysis.

✎ Correlation analysis contributes to the economic behaviour.

✎ It helps in locating the value of one variable on which others depend.

Methods of Studying Correlation

The methods used in the correlation analysis are the following.

    i.   Scatter diagram

    ii.   Correlation graph

    iii.   Karl Pearson's coefficient of correlation (r)

    iv.   Spearman's Rank correlation (r_{sp})

Scatter diagram   The first step in correlation analysis is always to draw a scatter diagram. It is a diagrammatic representation of bivariate data and is obtained by plotting the values of X and Y variables in the x–y plane. The diagram of dots so obtained is known as scatter diagram or scatter plot. From such a diagram we can have a fairly good idea as to whether the variables are correlated or not. For example, if the points are closely scattered, we expect a strong correlation between the variables. On the other hand, if the points are widely scattered, a poor or weak correlation or no correlation is expected between the variables.

The following are the different scatter diagrams when $r > 0$, $r < 0$, $r = 0$, and $r = \pm 1$.

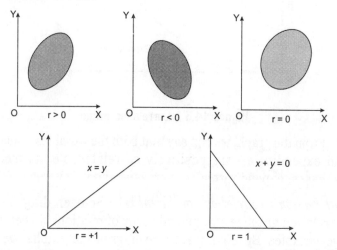

Figure 14.2 Scatter diagram showing relationship between two variables

Correlation graph This is specially used in the case of time series data, i.e., data collected and arranged over a period of time. While plotting the graph, time is taken along the x-axis and the values of the variable are taken along the y-axis. The values of each variable are plotted against the time in the x–y plane. The points are joined by a smooth curve. The curve so obtained is known as correlation graph. From the correlation graph, we can have a fairly good idea about the relationship existing between the variables. If both the curves proceed in the same direction, we say that the variables are positively correlated and vice-versa. However, with the help of this graph, we can only say whether the variables are related or not. We cannot quantify the degree or strength of the relationship through this diagram. An illustration of correlation graph is given below.

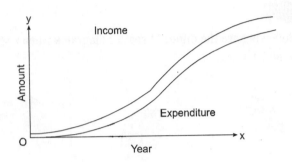

Figure 14.3   Correlation graph

From the graph, we can say that both the variables—income and expenditure—are positively correlated, i.e. as income increases, expenditure also increases and vice versa.

Karl Pearson's correlation coefficient (r)   Scatter diagram or correlation graph is a graphical study of relationship between two variables. By looking at these diagrams or graphs, we can have a rough idea about the relationship existing between the variables and the relationship cannot be measured numerically. Also, these methods cannot be used in the case of partial or multiple correlations. To overcome this problem, Karl Pearson devised a measure known as correlation index or correlation coefficient for quantifying the relationship between two or more variables. His index is denoted by 'r', the correlation coefficient. Below are given a few formulae for the computation of 'r'.

Formulae for computation of 'r'

i. $r = \dfrac{\Sigma xy}{\sqrt{\Sigma x^2}\sqrt{\Sigma y^2}}$ where, $x = X - \bar{X}, y = Y - \bar{Y}$ and x and y
are the deviations taken from and the actual means.

ii. $r = \dfrac{N\Sigma XY - (\Sigma X)(\Sigma Y)}{\sqrt{N\Sigma X^2 - (\Sigma X)^2}\sqrt{N\Sigma Y^2 - (\Sigma Y)^2}}$ where, X and Y are
the given values.

iii. $r = \dfrac{N\Sigma dxdy - (\Sigma dx)(\Sigma dy)}{\sqrt{N\Sigma dx^2 - (\Sigma dx)^2}\,\sqrt{N\Sigma dy^2 - (\Sigma dy)^2}}$ where, $dx = X - A$

$dy = Y - B$. A and B are assumed means. Here dx and dy are deviations taken from assumed means.

Limits for correlation coefficient

The correlation coefficient ranges between -1 and $+1$. If $r > 0$, the variables are positively correlated, and if $r < 0$, the variables are said to be negatively correlated. Further if $r = 0$, the variables are said to be uncorrelated.

Further if $r = +1$, the correlation is said to be perfect, i.e., the variables are linearly positively related and if $r = -1$, the variables are linearly negatively related.

Example

1. Calculate the coefficient of correlation (r) from the following data and comment on it.

X	9	8	7	6	5	4	3	2	1
Y	15	16	14	13	11	12	10	8	9

Solution

The formula for the calculation of correlation coefficient 'r' is given by:

$$r = \frac{\Sigma xy}{\sqrt{\Sigma x^2}\,\sqrt{\Sigma y^2}}$$

where,

$x = X - \bar{X}$ and
$y = Y - \bar{Y}$
$\bar{X}$ and $\bar{Y}$ are the means of X and Y

$$\bar{X} = \frac{\Sigma X}{n} = \frac{45}{9} = 5; \quad \bar{Y} = \frac{\Sigma Y}{n} = \frac{108}{9} = 12$$

X	Y	$x = X - \bar{X}$	$y = Y - \bar{Y}$	x^2	y^2	xy
9	15	4	3	16	9	12
8	16	3	4	9	16	12
7	14	2	2	4	4	4
6	13	1	1	1	1	1
5	11	0	−1	0	1	0
4	12	−1	0	1	0	0
3	10	−2	−2	4	4	4
2	8	−3	−4	9	16	12
1	9	−4	−3	16	9	12

$\Sigma X = 45 \quad \Sigma Y = 108 \quad \Sigma x = 0 \quad \Sigma y = 0 \quad \Sigma x^2 = 60 \quad \Sigma y^2 = 60 \quad \Sigma xy = 57$

Here $\Sigma x^2 = 60, \Sigma y^2 = 60, \Sigma xy = 57$

Substituting the values in the above formula, we get,

$$r = \frac{57}{\sqrt{60}\sqrt{60}} = \frac{57}{60} = 0.95$$

Comment

The strength or degree of relationship between the variables X and Y is +0.95. This implies that the variables X and Y are highly positively correlated. i.e., as X increases, variable Y also increases in the same direction.

2. Calculate the coefficient of correlation between experience (X) and performance (Y) from the following data and comment on it.

X	16	12	18	04	03	10	05	12
Y	23	22	24	17	19	20	18	21

Solution

$$r = \frac{N\Sigma dxdy - (\Sigma dx)(\Sigma dy)}{\sqrt{N\Sigma dx^2 - (\Sigma dx)^2}\sqrt{N\Sigma dy^2 - (\Sigma dy)^2}}$$

where,

$dx = X - A$,

$dy = Y - B$,

A and B are assumed means ($A = 10$ and $B = 20$)

X	Y	$dx = X - A$	$dy = Y - B$	dx^2	dy^2	$dxdy$
16	23	6	3	36	9	18
12	22	2	2	4	4	4
18	24	8	4	64	16	32
04	17	−6	−3	36	9	18
03	19	−7	−1	49	1	7
10	20	0	0	0	0	0
05	18	−5	−2	25	4	10
12	21	2	1	4	1	2
$\Sigma X = 80$	$\Sigma Y = 164$	$\Sigma dx = 0$	$\Sigma dy = 4$	$\Sigma dx^2 = 218$	$\Sigma dy^2 = 44$	$\Sigma dxdy = 91$

Here,

$$\Sigma dx = 0, \quad \Sigma dy = 4$$
$$\Sigma dx^2 = 218, \ \Sigma dy^2 = 44$$
$$\Sigma dxdy = 91, \ N = 8$$

Substituting these values in the above formula, we get

$$r = \frac{8 \times 91 - (0)(4)}{\sqrt{8 \times 218 - (0)^2}\sqrt{8 \times 44 - (4)^2}}$$

$$= \frac{728}{\sqrt{1744}\sqrt{352 - 16}}$$

$$= \frac{728}{\sqrt{1744}\sqrt{336}} = \frac{728}{41.76 \times 18.33}$$

$$= \frac{728}{765.46} = 0.95$$

Comment

The observed correlation coefficient is +0.95. This implies that the experience and performance of variables are highly positively correlated, i.e., as experience increases, performance also increases significantly in the same direction.

3. Find the coefficient of correlation between X and Y from the data given below. Comment on its value.

X	1	2	3	4	5	6	7	8	9
Y	9	8	7	6	5	4	3	2	1

Solution

$$r = \frac{N\Sigma XY - (\Sigma X)(\Sigma Y)}{\sqrt{N\Sigma X^2 - (\Sigma X)^2}\sqrt{N\Sigma Y^2 - (\Sigma Y)^2}}$$

X	Y	X^2	Y^2	XY
1	9	1	81	9
2	8	4	64	16
3	7	9	49	21
4	6	16	36	24
5	5	25	25	25
6	4	36	16	24
7	3	49	9	21
8	2	64	4	16
9	1	81	1	9
$\Sigma X = 45$	$\Sigma Y = 45$	$\Sigma X^2 = 285$	$\Sigma Y^2 = 285$	$\Sigma XY = 165$

Substituting these values in the above formula, we get,

$$r = \frac{9 \times 165 - (45)(45)}{\sqrt{9 \times 285 - (45)^2} \sqrt{9 \times 285 - (45)^2}}$$

$$= \frac{1485 - 2025}{\sqrt{2565 - 2025} \sqrt{2565 - 2025}}$$

$$= \frac{-540}{\sqrt{540} \sqrt{540}} = \frac{-540}{540} = -1$$

Comment

The observed correlation coefficient between the variables X and Y is -1. This shows that the variables X and Y are perfectly negatively correlated. That is, both the variables are proportionally changing in the opposite direction.

4. Calculate the coefficient of correlation "r" from the following data and comment on its value.

   Family income per day (Rs): 130 200 345 245 155 300 360 105
   080 275 225 095

   Weight of children   15.5 19.8 21.5 16.8 12.6 16.6 18.1 18.7
   (5 years of age) (kg):   13.1 20.1 18.1 17.4

   Using any one of the above formulae, the value of 'r' for this problem can be worked out as $r = 0.414$. This indicates a positive correlation between the variables, family income and weight of children, i.e., as income increases, weight of children also increases.

Coefficient of Determination (r^2)

This is a better measure than correlation coefficient in a bivariate analysis. It is obtained by squaring the value of r and multiplying with 100. It is expressed in percentage. This measures the proportion of the variation explained in the variable Y accounted by the variable X.

In the previous example, the value of *r* is 0.414 and its $r^2 = 0.1714$. Thus the coefficient of determination is 17.14%.

This implies that 17.14% of variation on weight is explained by the single independent variable, family income. Here weight is assumed to be a 'dependent variable'.

Interpreting the value of 'r'   How do you interpret each of the following values of '*r*' given below?

   r: + 1, – 1, –0.9 and +0.81.

Inference

1. When *r* = +1, the variables are perfectly positively related. This implies the proportionate change of the variables in the same direction.

2. When *r* = –1, the variables are perfectly negatively related. This implies the proportionate change of the variables in the opposite side.

3. When *r* = –0.9, it is inferred that the variables are highly negatively related to each other in the opposite direction.

4. When *r* = +0.81, it is inferred that the variables are highly positively related in the same direction.

Spearman's Rank Correlation (r_{sp})

Karl Pearson's coefficient of '*r*' is applicable only in the case of measurable characteristics or numerical measurements. For studying the relationship between two ordinal level measurements, Spearman's Rank correlation can be used. It is denoted by r_{sp}. The formula for the computation of r_{sp} (Rank correlation coefficient) is given by

$$r_{sp} = 1 - \frac{6 \Sigma D^2}{n(n^2 - 1)}$$

where,

$$D = R_x - R_y$$

R_x = Ranks in the X series

R_y = Ranks in the Y series

r_{sp} is interpreted in the same way as r. The values of r_{sp} range between -1 and $+1$.

Example

Seven participants were judged by 3 judges in a beauty competition. The ranks assigned by them are given below:

X	1	2	4	6	7	5	3
Y	2	1	4	5	6	7	3
Z	2	3	5	4	7	1	6

Which pair of judges were fair in their approach in assessing the beauty of the participants in the competition?

Solution

i.   Pair X and Y: Computation of r_{sp}.

$$r_{sp} = 1 - \frac{6\Sigma D^2}{n(n^2 - 1)}$$

where,

$$D = R_x - R_y$$

R_x = Ranks by X

R_y = Ranks by Y

R_x	R_y	$D = R_x - R_y$	D^2
1	2	−1	1
2	1	1	1
4	4	0	0
6	5	1	1
7	6	1	1
5	7	−2	4
3	3	0	0
			$\Sigma D^2 = 8$

$$r_{sp} = 1 - \frac{6\Sigma D^2}{n(n^2 - 1)}$$

$$= 1 - \frac{6 \times 8}{7(7^2 - 1)} = 1 - \frac{6 \times 8}{7 \times 48}$$

$$= 1 - \frac{48}{336} = 1 - 0.14 = 0.86 \tag{1}$$

ii. Pair X and Z: Computation of r_{sp}

R_x	R_z	$D = R_x - R_z$	D^2
1	2	−1	1
2	3	−1	1
4	5	−1	1
6	4	2	4
7	7	0	0
5	1	4	16
3	6	−3	9
			$\Sigma D^2 = 32$

$$r_{sp} = 1 - \frac{6\Sigma D^2}{n(n^2 - 1)}$$

$$= -1 - \frac{6 \times 32}{7 \times 48} = 1 - \frac{192}{336}$$

$$= 1 - 0.57 = 0.43 \tag{2}$$

iii. Pair Y and Z: Computation of r_{sp}.

R_y	R_z	$D = R_y - R_z$	D^2
2	2	0	0
1	3	−2	4
4	5	−1	1
5	4	1	1
6	7	−1	1
7	1	6	36
3	6	−3	9
			$\Sigma D^2 = 52$

$$r_{sp} = 1 - \frac{6\Sigma D^2}{n(n^2 - 1)}$$
$$= 1 - \frac{6 \times 52}{7 \times 48}$$
$$= 1 - \frac{312}{336}$$
$$= 1 - 0.93 = 0.07 \tag{3}$$

Inference

From 1, 2 and 3, we conclude that the judges X and Y were very fair in their approach in judging the beauty of the individuals who participated in the beauty competition.

REGRESSION ANALYSIS

Regression analysis is a statistical tool used to estimate the unknown values of a variable from the known values of another related variable. This is done by fitting a regression line with the observed data.

Uses of Regression Analysis

Regression analysis as a statistical tool is widely used in almost all the scientific disciplines. It is the basic technique for estimating the relationship between two variables. It provides estimates of values of the dependent variable from the values of the independent variable. It is also used to obtain a measure of the error involved in using the regression line as a basis for estimation. With the help of regression coefficients, we can also calculate the correlation coefficient.

Example

A survey was conducted on the family income and weight of 20 children of 5 years of age in an urban locality. The data obtained is given below. Perform regression analysis.

Daily family income (Rs.)	Weight (kg)	Daily family income (Rs.)	Weight (kg)
130	15.5	225	18.1
200	19.8	095	17.4
345	21.5	130	17.9
245	16.8	330	17.0
155	12.6	295	18.7
300	16.6	170	16.0
360	18.1	250	18.2
105	18.7	355	16.4
080	13.1	220	15.4
275	20.1	175	17.6

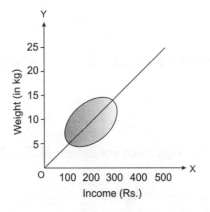

Scatter diagram of the given data

The scatter diagram above suggests that both weight and income are moving in the same direction implying a positive correlation between the variables, i.e., weight increases with an increase in family income. Thus, we can draw a line passing through these points as a simple measure of the relationship between the variables. This line is known as the regression line, which can also be used for estimation purpose.

Regression Line

Any straight line drawn on graph sheet can be represented by an equation given by

$$Y = a + bX$$

Each point on the line has an X value and a corresponding Y value. Also, the equation tells us how these X and Y values are related. For different values of a and b we can have different straight lines. The value of 'a' tells us the intercept of the line on the y-axis and 'b' is the slope of the line, and is also called the regression coefficient of Y on X. It represents the increment in the value of Y variable corresponding to a unit change in the

X variable. The value of *a* and *b* are obtained from the data given.

The regression coefficient of *Y* on *X* is denoted by 'b_{yx}' and is given by

$$b_{yx} = r\frac{\sigma y}{\sigma x}$$

Similarly, the regression coefficient of *X* on *Y* is given by

$$b_{xy} = r\frac{\sigma x}{\sigma y}$$

For the equation *Y* = *a* + *bX*, the values of *a* and *b* are also calculated as follows from the data given in the previous page.

$$b = \Sigma(X - \bar{X})(Y - \bar{Y}) / \Sigma(X - \bar{X})^2 \qquad (1)$$

$$a = \bar{Y} - b\bar{X} \qquad (2)$$

where,

    n is the number of values given

    $\bar{X}$ is the average of *X*-values

    $\bar{Y}$ is the average of *Y*-values

Example

1. From the data given below,

X	1	5	3	2	2	1	7	3
Y	6	1	0	0	1	2	1	5

a. Determine the regression line of *Y* on *X* and hence estimate *Y*, if *X* = 8

b. Determine the regression line of *X* on *Y* and hence estimate *X*, if *Y* = 15

X	Y	$X-\bar{X}$	$Y-\bar{Y}$	$(X-\bar{X})^2$	$(Y-\bar{Y})^2$	$(X-\bar{X})(Y-\bar{Y})$
1	6	-2	4	4	16	-8
5	1	2	-1	4	1	-2
3	0	0	-2	0	4	0
2	0	-1	-2	1	4	2
2	1	-1	-1	1	1	1
1	2	-2	0	4	0	0
7	1	4	-1	16	1	-4
3	5	0	3	0	9	0
24	16	0	0	30	36	-11

(a) To determine the regression line of Y and X:

The general form of the equation is given by

$$Y = a + bX$$

Here a and b are determined as follows:

$$a = \bar{Y} - b\bar{X} \qquad (1)$$

$$b = \frac{\sum(X-\bar{X})(Y-\bar{Y})}{\sum(X-\bar{X})^2} \qquad (2)$$

Substituting the values, we get,

$$b = \frac{-11}{30} = -0.367$$

$$\therefore a = 2 - (-0.367 \times 3)$$

$$= 2 + 1.101$$

$$= 3.101$$

$\therefore$ Regression equation is $Y = 3.101 - 0.367X$

When $X = 8$, $Y = 3.101 - 2.936 = 0.165$ units.

(b) Similarly, we can get $X = 3.612 - 0.306Y$ following the same procedure.

When $Y = 15$, $X = -0.06$ units.

Remarks

✎ A straight line should be fitted only if the scatter diagram suggests that the relationship between the two variables is roughly linear or significant.

✎ It is dangerous to extrapolate the regression line outside the range of the data.

Properties of Regression Coefficients

In the case of bivariate data, it is possible to have two regression equations, viz. regression equation of X on Y and regression equation of Y on X. These two regression coefficients will have the following properties.

✎ Both the regression coefficients will have the same sign.

✎ At least one of the regression coefficients will have value less than unity.

✎ The correlation coefficient will have the same sign as that of the regression coefficients.

✎ The square root of the product of the regression coefficients is the value of correlation coefficient between the variables under study.

TESTS OF SIGNIFICANCE

An important aspect of the sampling theory is the study of the test of significance. The test of significance helps us to decide on the basis of the sample results, if (i) the difference between the observed sample measures (such as mean, correlation coefficient, etc.) and population parameter value, or (ii) the difference between two sample measures is significant or due to chance or the fluctuations of sampling.

The conventional rules to be followed to test the significance of the difference are as follows:

✎ If the calculated probability is greater than 0.05 (P > 0.05), the difference is not significant at 5% level of significance.

✎ If the calculated probability is less than 0.05 (P ≤ 0.05), the difference is significant at 5% level of significance.

Similarly in the case of 1% level of significance, a significant value is the one whose associated probability of occurrence is less than or equal to the specified level of significance (generally 5% or 1% level of significance is chosen to reject the null hypothesis).

For the convenience of the researchers, different significance tests have been suggested for different sets of data and are given below in Table 14.13.

Table 14.13 Choosing a significance test to determine the significance of the difference between the groups*

Data level	Unpaired observations	Paired observations
Nominal data		
Small sample	Fischer's exact test	Sign test
Large sample	Chi-square test	Nc Nemar's χ^2-test
Ordinal data		
Two groups	Wilcoxon two-sample test or Mann-Whitney U-test, Kruskal-Wallis one-way ANOVA	Wilcoxon signed rank test, Friedman two-way ANOVA
More than two groups		
Interval ratio level data		
Two groups	t-test	Paired t-test
More than two groups	F-test	

*Source Reigelman, R.K. (1981). *Studying a study and testing a test*. Little Brown and Company, Boston, M.A. USA. p. 246.

Table 14.14 To determine the significance of the relationship/association between variables.

Nominal data	Chi-square test	Calculate odds ratio or estimate relative risk
Ordinal or numerical data when no linear relationship is suspected	Calculate Spearman's rho or Kendall's Tau	Significance of Spearman's rho or Kendall's Tau
Numerical data when a linear relationship is suspected	Calculate Karl Pearson's coefficient of correlation (r)	Significance of Pearson's correlation coefficient

While dealing with tabular analysis, particularly cross tabulations, we might have observed difference between groups. We may be interested in finding out if the difference is statistically significant or not.

To achieve this, we can perform the following two types of tests.

✎ t-test, and

✎ Chi-square test (χ^2)

TEST OF SIGNIFICANCE: t-TEST

The t-test is used for numerical data for comparing the means of two groups or two samples. The Chi-square test is used for categorical data while comparing proportions of events occurring in two or more groups. Both tests are used for unpaired observations. For paired observations, two different tests are used. They are discussed in the following pages.

Examples

1. In a survey of buying habits, 400 women shoppers were chosen at random in a supermarket 'A' located in a certain section of the city. Their average weekly food expenditure was Rs. 250 with an SD of Rs. 40. For 400 women shoppers chosen at random in the supermarket 'B' in another section of the city, the average weekly food expenditure was Rs. 220 with SD of Rs. 55. Test at 1% level of significance whether the average weekly food expenditure of the two population of shoppers are equal.

Calculation

Given:

$$n_1 = 400 \qquad \bar{X}_1 = Rs.250 \qquad S_1 = Rs.\ 40$$
$$n_2 = 400 \qquad \bar{X}_2 = Rs.220 \qquad S_2 = Rs.\ 55$$

Null Hypothesis (H_o): The average weekly food expenditure of the two populations of shoppers are equal.

The test statistic is given by

$$t = \frac{\bar{X}_1 - \bar{X}_2}{\sqrt{\dfrac{S_1^2}{n_1} + \dfrac{S_2^2}{n_2}}}$$

where

$\bar{X}_1$ - Mean expenditure of shoppers in supermarket A

$\bar{X}_2$ - Mean expenditure of shoppers in supermarket B

S_1 - SD of shoppers in A

S_2 - SD of shoppers in B

Substituting the values in the formula,

$$t = \frac{250 - 220}{\sqrt{\dfrac{40^2}{400} + \dfrac{55^2}{400}}}$$

$$= \frac{30}{\sqrt{4 + 7.5625}}$$

$$= \frac{30}{3.4003}$$

$$= 8.8228$$

Here the value of t is much greater than 3; the H_0 is rejected at 1% level of significance. We therefore conclude that the average weekly expenditure of the two population of shoppers differ significantly.

2. It has been observed that in a certain population of women, delivery through caesarean operation is very high. A study was conducted to discover the cause. As small height is known to be one of the risk factors related to difficult deliveries, the researcher wanted to find out if there was a significant difference between the mean height of women in the province who had normal deliveries and of those who had caesarean operation. The following results were obtained.

	No. of women	Mean height (in cm)	SD
Normal delivery	60	156	3.1
Caesarean operation	52	154	2.8

Test whether there is any significant difference between the mean height of women in the two categories.

Calculation

Given: $n_1 = 60$ $\overline{X}_1 = 156$ $S_1 = 3.1$

$n_2 = 52$ $\overline{X}_2 = 154$ $S_2 = 2.8$

Null Hypothesis (H_0): The two groups of women are the same with regard to their average height.

The test statistic is

$$t = \frac{\bar{X}_1 - \bar{X}_2}{\sqrt{\dfrac{S_1^2}{n_1} + \dfrac{S_2^2}{n_2}}}$$

Here

i. $\bar{X}_1 - \bar{X}_2 = 156 - 154 = 2$

ii. $S_1^2 / n_1 + S_2^2 / n_2 = 3.1^2 / 60 + (2.8)^2 / 52 = 0.56$

$$t = 2/\sqrt{0.56} = 3.6$$

Table value of t at 5% level of significance is 1.98. The calculated value of t is much greater than the table value of t and hence the difference is statistically significant. Therefore, hypothesis H_0 is rejected. That is, heightwise, women of the two groups are differing significantly.

❧❧❧❧❧❧❧❧

TEST OF SIGNIFICANCE: χ^2 - TEST

Examples

1. Two sample polls of votes for two candidates A and B for a public office are taken, one from among the residents of rural area and the other from an urban area. The results are given below. Examine whether there is any significant difference between rural and urban voters with regard to their voting preference.

Votes for area	A	B	Total
Rural	620	380	1000
Urban	550	450	1000
Total	1170	830	2000

Solution

Null Hypothesis (H_0): The nature of area is independent of the voting preference in the election.

The test statistic is $\chi^2 = \dfrac{\Sigma(O - E)^2}{E}$, where, O—observed frequencies E—expected frequencies.

Under the null hypothesis, the expected frequencies are calculated as follows:

E (620) = 1170 × 1000/2000 = 585

E (380) = 830 × 1000/2000 = 415

E (550) = 1170 × 1000/2000 = 585

E (450) = 830 × 1000/2000 = 415

Computation of χ^2-Value

O	E	O–E	$(O-E)^2$	$(O-E)^2/E$
620	585	35	1225	2.09
380	415	–35	1225	2.95
550	585	–35	1225	2.09
450	415	35	1225	2.95
				$\chi^2 = 10.08$

Inference

The tabulated χ^2 value for (2 – 1) (2 – 1) = 1 df at 5% level of significance is 3.84. The calculated value of χ^2 is much greater than the tabulated value, and is highly significant and hence the null hypothesis is rejected at 5% level of significance. Therefore, we conclude that the nature of area is related to voting preference in the election.

2. Regarding the utilization of antenatal clinics, it is observed that 64% of women who lived within 10 kms of the clinic came for antenatal care, as compared to only 47% of those who lived more than 10 kms away. This suggests that antenatal care (ANC) is often used by women who live close to the clinics. The results are given below:

Distance from ANC	Used ANC (%)	Did not use ANC (%)	Total (%)
Less than 10 km	51 (64)	29 (36)	80 (100)
10 km or more	35 (47)	40 (53)	75 (100)
Total	86	69	155

Test whether there is any significant difference between users and non-users of ANC.

Solution

Null Hypothesis (H_o): There is no difference between users and non-users of ANC with regard to distance.

The test statistic is $\chi^2 = \dfrac{\Sigma(O - E)^2}{E}$

where,

O—Observed frequencies and

E—Expected frequencies

The test is carried at 5% level of significance.

Computation of χ^2-value:

The expected frequencies are calculated as follows:

E (51) = 86 × 80/155 = 44.4

E (29) = 69 × 80/155 = 35.6

E (35) = 86 × 75/155 = 41.6

E (40) = 69 × 75/155 = 33.4

O	E	O–E	$(O–E)^2$	$(O–E)^2/E$
51	44.4	6.6	43.56	0.98
29	35.6	–6.6	43.56	1.22
35	41.6	–6.6	43.56	1.05
40	33.4	6.6	43.56	1.30
				$\chi^2 = 4.55$

Inference

The table value of χ^2 for 1 d.f at 5% level of significance is 3.84. The calculated value is more than the table value and hence H_o is rejected. Therefore, we conclude that the women within a distance of 10 km from the clinic use ANC frequently than those living more than 10 km away from ANC.

Note

- The test can be applied only if the sample is large enough, i.e., the total sample size should be at least 50 and the expected frequency in each cell should be at least 5.
- The test can also be used to compare more than two groups.

TEST OF SIGNIFICANCE: PAIRED *t*-TEST

While dealing with paired (matched) observations, comparison of means for significance is performed by a modified t-test known as the paired *t*-test.

In the case of paired observations, the test statistic *t* is given by

t = Mean difference/Standard error of difference.

Example

In a nutritional survey the following data was obtained. Compare the mean difference between the measurements of observer A and observer B at 5% level of significance.

In this case the number of df is $n-1$, where, n is the sample size.

Child No.	Weight measurement (kg)		Difference
	Observer A	Observer B	
1	18.6	17.7	0.9
2	17.1	14.5	2.6
3	14.3	12.4	1.9
4	23.2	20.7	2.5
5	18.4	16.8	1.6
6	14.9	14.4	0.5
7	16.6	14.1	2.5
8	14.8	17.1	–2.3
9	21.5	21.2	0.3
10	24.6	21.9	2.7
11	17.4	16.6	0.8
12	15.7	13.6	2.1
13	16.1	14.5	1.6
14	12.9	11.2	1.7
15	12.3	16.0	–3.7
16	19.4	20.4	–1.0
17	19.3	17.5	1.8
18	24.8	22.2	2.6
19	14.3	15.1	–0.8
20	13.4	10.9	2.5

Computation of test statistic (*t*)

Null Hypothesis (H_o): There is no significant difference between observer A and observer B with regard to weight measurements. The test statistic is

$$t = \text{Mean difference/SE}_r$$

Here

Mean difference = 1.04

Standard deviation of the difference = 1.77

Standard error $= SD / \sqrt{n} = 1.77 / \sqrt{20} = 0.40$

$\therefore t = 1.04 / 0.40 = 2.60$

The table value of *t* for 19 df at 5 % level of significance is 2.09.

Inference

The calculated value of t is more than the table value of *t* at 5% level of significance. This implies that the difference is significant. Hence H_0 is rejected and we conclude that there is a significant difference between the observers with regard to their weight measurements.

TESTING THE SIGNIFICANCE OF OBSERVED CORRELATION COEFFICIENT

To test whether the observed correlation coefficient is significant or not, we use the following test statistic.

$$t_c = \frac{r}{\sqrt{1-r^2}} \times \sqrt{n-2}$$

Here

r—observed correlation coefficient, and

n—number of pairs of observations

Further, t is based on $(n-2)$ df.

The calculated t-value is compared with the tabulated t-value and the inference is drawn.

For example, if $r = 0.414$, and $n = 20$, we have

$$t_c = \frac{0.414}{\sqrt{1-(0.414)^2}} \times \sqrt{20.2}$$

$$= \frac{0.414}{\sqrt{0.8286}} \times \sqrt{18}$$

$$= \frac{0.414}{0.9103} \times 4.2426$$

$$= 1.9295$$

Here table value of 't' at 5% level of significance for 18 df. is 2.10.

Since the calculated value of t is less than the table value of t, the observed correlation coefficient is not significant. This implies that the relation is not significant at 5% level of significance.

15
REPORT WRITING

INTRODUCTION

The essence of all research studies is the preparation and presentation of the research report. A research report is a formal statement of the research process and its results. It narrates the research problem methods used for studying it, and the findings and conclusions of the study.

The purpose of a research report is

1. to disseminate amongst the interested people, the knowledge that has been acquired through study of a problem or research.
2. to present the conclusions for the information and knowledge of others.
3. to check the validity of the generalizations.
4. to encourage others to carry on research on the same or allied problems.

CHARACTERISTICS OF A GOOD REPORT

A good report is expected to possess the following.

Attractiveness   A report should be neatly typed on good paper and contain neat diagrams and graphs. The title cover should be attractive with needed information.

Balanced language   The language should be simple, standard, technical and befitting the subject described.

No repetition of facts   It adds to the bulk of the report and makes the reader bored.

Statement of scientific facts   The facts given in the report should be scientific and not imaginary. The analysis and presentation of data should be highly valid and reliable.

Practicability   The suggestions given should be practical and only then may be implemented.

Description of the difficulties and the shortcomings   If the difficulties and shortcomings of the study are concealed, the future researchers also may not be able to overcome them and cannot give correct findings.

FORMAT AND CONTENTS OF A RESEARCH REPORT

A broad sequence of contents is given here. It may vary from institution to institution.

A research report contains three parts

1. The preliminary pages
2. The text or body of the report
3. The reference material

The preliminary section includes

i. the title page
ii. researcher's declaration
iii. the certificate of the research supervisor
iv. acknowledgements
v. table of contents
vi. list of tables

vii. list of figures and illustrations and

viii. abstract or synopsis

The text or body of a report consists of

i. introduction

ii. research design

iii. results, findings and discussion

iv. summary and conclusion

The reference material consists of

i. bibliography

ii. appendices

iii. glossary of terms (if any)

iv. index (if any)

Preliminary Section

Title page Title page should include

- the title of the research study
- the name of the degree for which it is submitted
- the name of the researcher
- the name of the institute where the research work is to be submitted
- the date of submission of the report

Researcher's declaration In the case of a research work undertaken by a student in fulfilment of the requirements of a degree, they may be required to make a declaration as given in the box.

DECLARATION

I, Smt. G. Vijayalakshmi, declare that the thesis entitled "Factors Influencing Adoption of Appropriate Health Technologies by Rural Women" is the bonafide record of the independent research work carried out by me under the supervision and guidance of Prof. A. Suriakanthi. This has not been submitted earlier elsewhere for the award of any diploma, degree or fellowship.

Gandhigram   G. Vijayalakshmi
14.3.96.

The certificate of the research supervisor   In the case of a student's research work, the research supervisor has to certify that it is a record of independent research work done by the student as given in the box below.

CERTIFICATE

I certify that the thesis entitled "Factors Influencing Adoption of Appropriate Health Technologies by Rural Women" is the bonafide record of independent research work carried out by Smt. G. Vijayalakshmi under my supervision and guidance. This has not been submitted earlier for the award of any diploma, degree or fellowship.

Gandhigram   A. Suriakanthi
14.3.96.   Research Supervisor

Acknowledgements Here, the researcher acknowledges the assistance and support received from individuals and institutions in conducting the research. It is intended to show his/her gratitude. The comments given in acknowledgements should be brief, simple and modest and given only when substantial assistance was received from the individuals.

Table of contents   The purpose of table of contents is to provide an outline of the content of the report. It may contain only a list of titles of chapters followed by page number on which each chapter begins and ends.

List of tables   This comes after the "table of contents". All the tables may be numbered serially as 1, 2, 3, 4, 5 in one series, or tables in each chapter may be given in a separate serial order as 1.1, 1.2, 1.3 for tables in chapter 1, and so on. Both tables and figures may be given on the same page.

List of figures and illustrations   These are synonymous terms and it refers to graphs, diagrams, drawings and photographs.

Abstract   It is placed at the begining of the report so that a reader can have a quick overview of the report. It contains a brief statement of the need and scope of the study and the study design used for investigation, and a summary of the findings. It should be brief and about one or two pages.

Text or Body of the Report

The text is the major part of the report. The text usually consists of the following.

Introduction   The introduction includes

- the theoretical background of the research topic
- the statement of the problem with a conceptual framework
- review of available information and studies conducted in this field
- need and scope of the study
- the objectives and hypotheses of the study
- definition of concepts

Research process   This is the heart of the research report covering all aspects of research methodology, sample design, data collection instruments, methods of data processing and plan of analysis and limitations of the study. If a pilot study was conducted, how the outcome of the pilot study was utilized for designing the final study should be stated.

Results and discussion   The report should be highly organized and divided depending on the number of objectives of the study, each being devoted for presenting the results pertaining to an objective. Each section may have an appropriate heading with the following details.

- A brief description of the accepted principle/theory.
- A citation of previous relevant and significant studies.
- Presentation of the summary table.
- Presentation of the findings and the inference. The presentation should not be in isolation. They should lead logically to the succeeding sections. Phrases like "As given in the table or as shown in the above table" should be avoided as far as possible.

The divisions should be well balanced, related and arranged in a logical sequence.

Every table should be self-contained and self-explanatory and the presentation should be clear. To support or contradict the findings, the researcher can quote studies done by other experts in that field and say whether the hypothesis is accepted or rejected.

A model for presentation of results is given below:

DEMOGRAPHIC CHARACTERISTICS AND FAMILY PLANNING ADOPTION

Family composition and access to health centres are likely to influence the adoption of family planning methods. Somajulu (1992) observed in his study a rapid increase in the proportion of users of contraceptive methods among mothers having both male and female children and among those having easy access to health centres.

Table 15.1   Family composition and adoption of family planning method

Demographic characteristics	No. of mothers (n = 500)	Family planning methods		
		Non-adopters	Adopters	Total
Family composition				
All boys	163	58.5	41.5	100
All girls	154	66.9	33.1	100
Boys = girls	102	39.2	30.8	100
Boys more	38	36.8	63.2	100
Girls more	43	58.8	44.2	100
		P < 0.01		
Access to health facilities				
Stratum I	210	51.0	49.0	100
Stratum II	290	57.9	42.1	100

Stratum I—Villagers with easy access to health centres.

Stratum II—Villagers away from health centres.

Proportion of family planning adopters are more among mothers having more number of boys or equal number of boys and girls (Table 15.1).

To test the significance of this association, Chi square test was applied. The relationship between family composition and adoption of family planning methods among mothers was statistically significant.

$$(\chi_c^2 = 83.89, df = 4, p < 0.01)$$

But the relationship of adopters with their access to health centres was not significant, showing that there is no relationship between family planning adopters and their access to health centres. This may be due to other factors like their family composition, child mortality, their knowledge and attitude on contraceptives.

As stated above, negative results also should be stated with explanations. Each table or chapter should have a summary and lead into the next chapter with smooth coherence.

Summary, conclusion and recommendations The summary is a brief review of the entire work from the problem to the principle. The summary may be more or less a restatement of the topical sentences of the various findings presented in the main body.

Conclusions are answers to the questions raised or the statements of acceptance or rejection of the hypotheses proposed. A researcher should not generalize certain findings based on his/her limited data and not tested by the analysis.

Recommendations should be specific and should not be vague. Suggestions must be practicable based on logical reasoning taking into consideration all the difficulties that may arise in implementing them.

Reference Material

The bibliography The bibliography is a list of references relating to a subject or topic. It is placed at the end of the main body of the report. The bibliography may be limited to only those works that is found significantly relevant or can include all works that were consulted in the preparation of the report and that had any bearing on the topic.

Purpose of bibliography Bibliography enables the interested reader to pursure the problem further and also to verify the facts and statements in the report. It also adds weight to the report by indicating the depth and extensiveness of the work done. The purpose of bibliography is different from that of footnotes. The differences are as follows:

- ✎ The footnotes designate the exact place or page number where the cited matter is located. But the bibliography just gives identification details for the works, as a whole.

- ✎ There may be several footnotes to a work, but there is only one entry for it in a bibliography.

- ✎ The footnote is given only when a specific matter from a work is cited, whereas a reference may be listed in the bibliography even if it is not quoted in the report, provided, it is related to the subject of the study.

- ✎ No page number is stated in the case of books and reports listed in the bibliography.

- ✎ In the footnote for the work, author's first name is given first whereas in bibliography, the author's last name is given.

Classification   The length of the bibliography will determine the basic classification. In a comparatively short bibliography, all works will be listed under a single heading. In longer ones, the references are arranged under separate subheadings like books, periodicals, reports and articles.

Bibliographical entries are arranged alphabetically by author's last name. Where no author is listed, the work is listed by the first word of the title exclusive of any article (a, and, the) and the article is listed following the title.

Contents of bibliographical entries

1. The author's last name followed by a comma; the first name and middle initial, followed by a period.

2. The title of the work, followed by a period. Titles of full length works are italicized.

3. The edition number, followed by a period.

4. The name of the compiler, editor followed by a period.

5. The place of publication followed by a colon. If the city is not well known, the state should also appear. When more than one place of publication is given in the book, generally the first one is used.

6. The name of the publisher, followed by a comma.

7. The year of publication, followed by a period. If the date of publication does not appear on the title page but has been located elsewhere, it should be enclosed within brackets. If it cannot be located, then the approximate copyright date is given with the notation C. (circa), e.g. C. 1986. When neither date of publication nor copyright date is available, the notation n.d. (no date) is listed.

Examples

1. *Book written by one author*

   Mann, M.K. *Home Management for Indian Families*, 4th edn. Ludhiana: Kalyani Publishers, 2004.

2. *Book written by two authors*

   Boyer, Ernest, L. and Boyer, Paul. *Smart Parents' Guide to College*. Princeton, New Jersey: Peterson's, 1996.

3. *Book written by more than three authors*

   Varghese, M.A. *et al*. *Home Management*. New Delhi: Wiley Eastern Limited, C. 1985.

   More than one book by the same author. Repetition of his name is avoided by substituting for it an unbroken line eight spaces in length, beginning with the left margin.

4. *Journal articles*

   Baradha, G and Niranjana, S. "Enhancing self concept among slow learners." *Journal of Extension and Research*, Vol VIII. Nos. 1 and 2, 2006, pp. 61–65.

5. *Newspaper*

   The Hindu, February 19, 2004, p. 5.

6. *Newspaper* (Title and author given)

   Shareefa. "Good start to the day." *The Hindu, Young World*. December 11, 2004, p. 1.

7. *Report*

   World Bank, World Development Report 1987, Washington D.C., 1987.

8. *Bulletin* (Institution or organization as author)

   i. Ministry of Health and Family Welfare, 1992–1993.

   ii. Bulletin on Rural Health Statistics in India, New Delhi: Government of India, 1992.

Spacing   All bibliographical entries are single-spaced with double spaces between entries. The authors last name begins at margin and where the entry contains more than one line, successive lines are indented. The same indentation should be observed for all entries.

Appendices   Appendices include

- copies of data collection instruments (interview schedules or questionnaires)
- technical details of sampling
- statistical computations

Glossary of terms   An alphabetical list of words relating the report with needed explanations may be given.

Index   Index may be subject index or author index. The index, if prepared, should give an alphabetically arranged, detailed reference to all important matters discussed in the report, such as names of persons, places, events, definitions, concepts and vital statements.

FOOTNOTES

Footnotes are conventional procedures which should be used sparingly and only when the material being presented clearly needs amplification or acknowledgement. There are a number of guidelines that can be followed for appropriate footnoting.

Use of Footnotes

In the interest of scholarly honesty, the source or authority should be acknowledged through the use of a footnote. Footnotes are used to

- validate a point, statement or argument.
- explain, supplement or amplify material that is included in the main body of the paper.
- provide cross-references to other sections.
- acknowledge a direct quotation or indirect quotation.
- provide the reader with sufficient information to enable him to consult sources independently.
- to give the original version of the material that has been translated in the text.

Footnote Contents

The first time a work is cited, it must include all the information necessary for easy location of the work. It should include the author's full name, the title of the work, the facts of the publication and the volume and page numbers. This information should be arranged as follows.

1. Author's first name, middle initial and last name, followed by a comma.
2. Title of the book, underlined.

3. Place and date of publication separated by a comma and enclosed in parentheses, followed by a comma.

4. Volume number, in large roman numerals, followed by a comma.

5. Page number followed by a period.

Placement and Numbering of Footnotes

Footnotes may be placed

1. at the foot of a page
2. at the end of a chapter
3. at the end of a paper

Placement at the bottom is preferred. A footnote citation is indicated by placing a superscript number at the point of reference. Superscript number may be confusing for mathematical formulae. In such cases, symbols like asterisk (*) may be used. The superscript numeral must appear at the top of the line both in the text and in a footnote. No mark of punctuation is used after the superscript numeral, either in the text or in a footnote. Where the paper is not divided into chapters, footnotes should be numbered consecutively throughout.

Conventions in Footnoting

Use of ibid When references to the same work follow each other without any intervening reference, even though they are separated by several pages, the abbreviation *ibid* ("in the same place") is used to repeat the preceding reference. Any changes in volume and/or page number(s) must be indicated following *ibid*. If the reference is to the same volume and page number as the preceding reference, nothing follows *ibid*.

[1]Stella Soundararaj. *A Text Book of Household Arts*, 4th edn. (New Delhi, 1996) pp. 37–38.

∞∞∞∞∞∞∞∞

This is the first and therefore complete reference to the work.

[2]*Ibid*

Since there are no intervening references, the second mention of the work requires only *ibid*. When the second footnote refers to the same page, pp. 37–38, no page numbers need to be indicated.

[3]*Ibid.*, p. 40

Since there have been no intervening references, *ibid* is still correct; but this time it refers to a different page. So as long as there are no intervening references, *ibid* may continue to be used.

Use of op. cit.

If the same work already cited in full form, is cited after one or more references from other publication, then we should include author's last name and the abbrevation op.cit. ("in the work cited") and the page numbers. Some examples of these usages are given below:

1. Sunita Borkar. *A Text Book of Applied Art.* Mumbai, 2003. p. 87.

2. Bharathi, V.V. and Jacintha, M. *Family Resource Management.* New Delhi, 1994. p. 35.

3. Borkar, op.cit., p. 95. (Since there was an intervening reference, op.cit. must be used and the new page designated.)

Use of loc.cit. Loc.cit. ("in the place cited") is used in lieu of *ibid*, when the reference is not only to the work immediately preceding but also refers to the same page. Loc.cit. is also used in lieu of op.cit. when reference is made to a work previously cited and to the same page in that work. Hence loc.cit. is never followed by volume and/or page numbers. When it takes the place of *ibid*, loc. cit is capitalized.

Examples

[1]Pramila Mebra, *Interior Decoration*, 3rd edn. New Delhi, 1981. p. 46.

[2]M.K. Mann. *Home Management for Indian Families*, 4th edn. Ludhiana, 2004. p.63.

[3]*Ibid*., p 70.

Note

If the reference was to the same page, then loc.cit. would have been used.

[4]Mebra, *loc.cit*

(Note: Loc.cit is used to refer to p. 46.)

EDITING AND EVALUATION

Report writing is not an easy task. Researchers may come across the following problems.

1. *The problem of communication.*

   ✎ The purpose of a research report is to communicate information to the reader.

✎ The technical terms should be properly explained and should be clear to the reader.

✎ It should not be too simple or too difficult to understand.

✎ The report should take into consideration the "needs of the audience" for whom it is meant.

✎ The language used should be neither too colloquial nor too scholarly. The report should not be a mere collection of facts nor should it be written in a flowery language.

2. *The problem of objectivity.* The report should be free from prejudices and biases and should have no place for exaggerations.

3. *The problem of expression of unpleasant facts.* Bitter and unpleasant facts should be presented in such a way that they neither injure the feelings of a particular group nor cause harm for any other group. The researcher has to be cautious in giving facts which cannot be proved but believed as to be true, for the sake of fellow researchers.

Evaluation of a Research Report

There is no universally accepted set of standards for evaluating a research report. However, the following checklist (Table 15.2) will serve as the guideline for analysis of a research report.

Table 15.2 Research report evaluation format

	Yes	No		Yes	No
I. Title			Assumptions stated		
Precise and clear			Important terms defined		
Specific			**III. Review of literature**		
Appropriate			Adequately covered		
II. Introduction			Well organized		
Problem			Recent studies given		
Relevant			**IV. Research design**		
Significant			Appropriate study design		
Clearly stated			Variables relevant to objectives		
Hypothesis			Good data collection techniques		
Clearly stated			Effective data gathering tools		
Testable			Representative sample		
Significance recognized			Adequate sample		
Properly delimited					

V. Data analysis
- Desired data
- Effective use of tables
- Effective use of figures
- Findings-well organized
- Appropriate statistical tests
- Good interpretation
- Logical analysis

VI. Summary
- Problem restated
- Questions/hypothesis restated
- Procedure described
- Findings concisely presented
- Conclusions based on data analysis
- Judicious recommendation
- Suggested further research

VII. Form and style
- Correct placement of table of contents
- List of figures
- Bibliography
- Appendix
- Typing
- Proper spacing
- Punctuation
- Spelling
- Margin
- Pagination
- Proper arrangement of
- Heading
- Bibliography
- Footnotes
- Tables
- Quotations
- Balanced language

	1	2	3	4	5	6	7	8	9	10	11	12	13	14	15	16	17	18	19	20	21	22	23	24	25	26	27	28	29	30	31	32
1	8	0	9	4	2	5	2	5	8	2	4	7	1	3	4	7	7	4	3	8	3	6	2	0	1	8	9	7	2	1	3	4
2	3	5	6	3	2	1	9	8	8	7	1	1	9	0	4	5	2	6	1	8	3	7	5	1	2	6	2	6	1	0	9	5
3	1	3	0	0	6	3	3	1	3	2	5	3	9	6	9	3	8	7	3	0	2	8	1	5	1	5	3	8	8	5	4	3
4	3	5	6	5	0	0	1	6	2	5	4	3	6	4	3	2	4	7	9	6	6	0	9	5	5	2	8	3	1	6	2	0
5	7	8	5	0	5	9	2	5	5	7	8	8	7	3	1	1	2	1	9	2	6	8	4	8	3	5	3	0	5	5	8	9
6	4	4	9	0	5	4	1	7	9	3	2	7	6	1	5	3	5	9	0	1	4	7	7	5	9	9	8	0	9	8	7	7
7	6	5	4	5	9	1	0	4	1	2	1	8	8	8	1	9	7	5	3	1	4	3	8	0	9	3	7	3	2	4	4	5
8	3	6	2	6	5	9	9	5	7	5	1	5	9	7	5	3	9	5	2	8	2	6	5	8	2	9	4	4	1	8	9	9
9	4	6	6	5	4	8	2	0	0	4	5	4	0	6	1	2	9	2	8	3	5	4	5	1	0	1	3	8	4	7	0	0
10	6	4	9	8	7	5	1	0	9	3	7	1	7	8	1	8	6	6	3	2	4	6	5	3	9	8	7	2	8	0	9	4
11	6	7	2	2	9	8	6	9	5	1	6	5	7	8	7	5	4	8	8	3	9	1	8	5	0	0	1	0	4	8	3	2
12	9	7	4	0	5	9	3	9	1	4	1	9	2	7	2	1	0	8	3	6	3	3	0	3	9	6	1	3	5	0	1	9
13	5	6	4	8	1	4	1	2	8	8	1	0	7	4	3	4	8	0	6	9	1	9	1	8	0	7	9	8	9	0	3	6
14	7	4	4	1	9	2	0	7	4	6	4	2	5	8	8	4	4	1	9	3	9	6	0	0	1	2	2	9	6	3	3	0
15	8	2	7	4	3	0	1	0	1	0	7	4	3	7	4	2	3	3	7	2	7	1	6	4	9	1	8	1	2	9	9	2
16	0	1	6	9	7	6	1	9	7	5	2	5	2	3	8	3	2	9	9	3	3	7	0	9	9	0	9	5	9	4	8	0
17	7	3	8	1	9	7	5	7	3	6	5	5	6	6	2	7	9	8	7	5	4	7	8	7	1	5	3	6	2	7	4	7
18	9	8	3	8	4	7	1	9	6	5	9	6	2	9	1	4	1	9	0	0	6	5	7	8	5	5	0	4	0	5	9	8
19	1	8	8	0	4	2	1	4	8	5	2	9	4	5	3	9	8	8	3	1	2	7	0	4	1	0	4	5	0	7	6	3
20	3	2	6	7	2	5	1	6	7	6	6	4	2	3	1	5	3	4	3	2	4	5	5	0	9	6	5	1	7	3	5	5
21	4	9	4	1	4	9	3	0	1	2	3	0	2	5	4	0	6	9	5	8	5	4	8	3	9	8	4	5	4	7	9	6
22	1	5	5	7	8	1	0	6	2	3	5	3	2	3	0	3	1	2	0	0	8	7	0	5	2	0	3	4	6	5	2	2
23	8	3	5	0	9	6	9	7	8	4	8	7	6	9	7	4	6	1	1	1	7	2	0	8	9	1	1	8	7	5	5	6
24	7	9	4	4	5	8	2	3	6	9	8	8	0	4	5	6	3	1	2	8	9	7	6	1	2	0	6	7	2	6	6	9
25	6	7	7	6	9	9	4	7	8	4	7	2	8	2	7	0	9	7	8	3	4	5	0	6	1	7	1	7	0	6	7	1
26	7	9	1	0	6	0	0	3	8	4	4	1	2	7	8	3	1	5	1	9	4	8	1	0	5	5	8	5	4	8	6	2
27	2	9	5	9	2	3	1	8	2	1	3	7	6	5	0	2	9	9	8	8	2	4	6	7	3	8	6	8	9	0	6	3
28	9	2	4	1	0	8	9	2	9	3	0	5	5	0	4	2	7	3	0	3	3	9	8	9	1	0	9	9	1	7	6	1
29	4	5	8	4	7	4	1	6	9	6	6	5	6	2	4	5	1	1	8	9	5	9	1	6	9	0	9	8	6	5	7	4
30	4	6	1	3	8	5	4	9	6	3	6	9	3	2	0	8	5	1	0	9	9	6	8	0	1	5	6	8	6	1	3	3

How to use random numbers table

- ✎ Decide the size of the sample, either two or larger digit number.

- ✎ Decide whether to go across the page to the right, or left, down the page or up the page in the table.

- ✎ Without looking at the table, using a pencil, pen, stick or finger, pinpoint a number.

- ✎ If the number is within the range needed, one can take it. If not, continue to the next number in the direction one chose beforehand, until one finds a number that is within the range. For example, if we need a number 0–50 and if we began at column 21, 22, row 21 we will get 74 which is obviously too big. So we could go down to 97, also too big, to 42, which is acceptable and select it.

APPENDIX 2

SIGNIFICANT VALUES OF t FOR GIVEN PROBABILITIES

Degrees of freedom	Probability, p		
	0.05	0.01	0.001
1	12.71	63.66	636.62
2	4.30	9.93	31.60
3	3.18	5.84	12.92
4	2.78	4.60	8.61
5	2.57	4.03	6.87
6	2.45	3.71	5.96
7	2.37	3.50	5.41
8	2.31	3.36	5.04
9	2.26	3.25	4.78
10	2.23	3.17	4.59
11	2.20	3.11	4.44
12	2.18	3.06	4.32
13	2.16	3.01	4.22
14	2.14	2.98	4.14
15	2.13	2.95	4.07
16	2.12	2.92	4.02
17	2.11	2.90	3.97
18	2.10	2.88	3.92
19	2.09	2.86	3.88
20	2.09	2.85	3.85
21	2.08	2.83	3.82

(Contd.)

Degrees of freedom	Probability, p		
	0.05	0.01	0.001
22	2.07	2.82	3.79
23	2.07	2.81	3.77
24	2.06	2.80	3.75
25	2.06	2.79	3.73
26	2.06	2.78	3.71
27	2.05	2.77	3.69
28	2.05	2.76	3.67
29	2.05	2.76	3.66
30	2.04	2.75	3.65
40	2.02	2.70	3.55
60	2.00	2.66	3.46
120	1.98	2.62	3.37
∞	1.96	2.58	3.29

APPENDIX 3

SIGNIFICANT VALUES OF x^2

Degrees of freedom	Probability		
	0.05	**0.01**	**0.0001**
1	3.84	6.64	10.83
2	5.99	9.21	13.82
3	7.82	11.35	16.27
4	9.49	13.28	18.47
5	11.07	15.09	20.52
6	12.59	16.81	22.46
7	14.07	18.48	24.32
8	15.51	20.09	26.13
9	16.92	21.67	27.88
10	18.31	23.21	29.59
11	19.68	24.73	31.26
12	21.03	26.22	32.91
13	22.36	27.69	34.53
14	23.69	29.14	36.12
15	25.00	30.58	37.70
16	26.30	32.00	39.25
17	27.59	33.41	40.79
18	28.87	34.81	42.31
19	30.14	36.19	43.82
20	31.41	37.57	45.32

(Contd.)

Degrees of freedom	Probability		
	0.05	0.01	0.0001
21	32.67	38.93	46.80
22	33.92	40.29	48.27
23	35.17	41.64	49.73
24	36.42	42.98	51.18
25	37.65	44.31	52.62
26	38.89	45.64	54.05
27	40.11	46.96	55.48
28	41.34	48.28	56.89
29	42.56	49.59	58.30
30	43.77	50.89	59.70

SELECTED BIBLIOGRAPHY

Devadas, Rajammal, P. (eds.). *A Handbook on Methodology of Research.* Coimbatore: Sri Ramakrishna Mission Vidhyalaya Press. 1969.

Gupta, S.C. and Kapoor, V.K. *Fundamentals of Mathematical Statistics.* New Delhi: Sultan Chand and Sons. 1977.

Jain Lal, Gopal, *Research Methodology.* Jaipur: Mangal Deep Publications. 1998.

Kothari, C.R. *Research Methodology: Methods and Techniques.* New Delhi: Wiley Eastern Ltd. 1988.

Krishnaswami, O.R. and Ranganathan, M. *Methodology of Research in Social Sciences.* Mumbai: Himalaya Publishing House. 2005.

Misra, B.N. and Misra, M.K. *Introducing Practical Biostatistics.* Calcutta: Darbari Udjog. (C) 1983.

Ray, G.L. and Mondal Sagar. *Research Methods in Social Sciences and Extension Education.* Calcutta: Naya Prokash. 1999.

Saravanavel, P. *Research and Report Writing.* Chennai: Emerald Publishers. 1985.

Sidhu Singh Kulbir. *Methodology of Research in Education.* New Delhi: Sterling Publishers. 1984.

Teitelbaum, Harry. *How to Write a Thesis,* 5th. edn. New Delhi: Goyal Publishers. (C) 1966.

Varkevisser, Corlien, M. Pathmanathan, Indra and Brownlee Ann. *Designing and Conducting Health Systems Research Projects.* Vol 2, Part - 1. International Development Research Centre, Ottawa, Canada. (C) 1991.

Varkevisser, Corlien M. *et al. Designing and conducting Health Systems Research Projects*. Vol 2, Part 2. Ottawa: International Development Research Centre. (C) 1991.

William, Goods. J. and Halt, Paul, K. *Methods in Social Research*. New York: McGraw-Hill International Book Company. 1981.

Yadava, S.S. and Yadava, K.N.S. *Satistical Analysis for Social Sciences*. New Delhi: Manas Publications. 1995.

INDEX

A

Accidental sampling 95
Acknowledgements 191
Analysis 111
Appendices 198
Applicability 18
Arithmetic average 134
Arithmetic mean 134
Attitude scales 75
Average 133, 134

B

Bar diagrams 121
Bias 96
Bibliography 195
Brief description 22

C

Categorical data 58, 112, 113
Categorizing 108
Central measure 133, 142
Central values 142
Certificate 190
Checklist 62, 63
Chi-square test 176
Closed-form
    questionnaire 70, 71
Cluster sampling 93
Coding 109
Coefficient of determination 165
Coefficient of range 143

Coefficient of variation 133
Column percentage 128
Combined average 140
Combined standard deviation 145
Concise description 22
Conclusions 195
Concurrent validity 82
Confidence interval 153, 154
Confidence limits 153
Construct validity 82
Content validity 82
Continuous variable 113, 114
Convenience sampling 94
Correlation 133
Correlation analysis 155, 158
Correlation coefficient 161, 170
Correlation graph 158, 159
Cross tables 126
Cross tabulation 129

D

Data 53
Data collection 198
Data collection techniques 59, 79
Data processing 107
Dependent variables 111
Depth interviews 65
Description 22
Descriptive variables 108
Discrete variable 113, 114
Document schedule 73

E

Editing 108, 202
Equivalent form method 81
Evaluation 203

F

Face validity 82
Feasibility 18
Focus group discussion 79, 80
Focused interviews 65
Footnotes 196, 199, 200
Frequency
    distribution 113, 114, 116
Frequency table 127

G

Geometric mean 134
Glossary of terms 198

H

Harmonic mean 134
Histogram 121, 123

I

ibid 200, 201, 202
Independent variable 112
Index 198
Interval 112
Interview 67
Interviewing 64
Interview schedule 73

J

Judgement sampling 94

K

Karl Pearson's correlation
    coefficient 158, 160, 166

L

Line graph 121, 125
Linear correlation 157
Linker's method 76, 77
Linker-type scale 78
loc.cit. 202

M

Mean 133, 134
Mean deviation 133
Measure of central
    tendency 133, 142
Measures of kurtosis 133
Measures of skewness 133
Median 133, 135
Mode 133, 136
Moving average 134
Multi-stage sampling 92
Multiple correlation 133, 157
Multiple regression 133

N

Negative correlation 156
Nominal 112
Nominal characteristic 114
Non-directive interview 65
Non-linear correlation 157
Non-participant observation 61
Non-probability sampling 94
Non-structured interviews 65
Non-structured questionnaire 70
Normal distribution 150
Null hypothesis 179
Numerical data 58, 113
Numerical variables 113

O

Objectivity 80, 84
Observation 60, 62

Observation schedule 73
op.cit. 201
Open-ended
   questionnaire 70, 71
Ordinal 112
Ordinal characteristic 115
Ordinal data 58

P

Paired *t*-test 182
Partial correlation 133, 157
Partial regression 133
Participant observation 60
Percentages 116
Pie diagram 121, 123
Positional average 135
Positive correlation 155
Practicability 80, 83, 188
Predictive validity 82
Primary data 53
Probability sampling 88
Processing data 108
Progressive average 134
Proportion 117

Q

Qualitative data 56
Qualitative research
   techniques 80
Quantitative data 56, 58
Quartile deviation 133
Questionnaire 68, 70
Quota sampling 95

R

Range 133, 143, 144
Rank correlation coefficient 166
Rate 119

Rating scale 62
Rating schedule 73
Ratio level 112
Ratios 118
Recommendations 195
Regression
   analysis 155, 169, 170
Regression coefficient 171, 174
Regression line 171
Relative frequencies 116
Reliability 80, 81, 83
Repeatability 81
Repetitive interviews 65
Report writing 202
Representative sample 86
Reproducibility 81
Research process 193
Research report 187
Row percentage 128

S

Sample 87, 89
Sample size 97
Sampling 85, 86, 87
Sampling technique 87
Scatter diagram 121, 126, 158
Schedule 72, 74
Score-card 62, 63
Secondary data 54, 55
Simple classification 56
Simple correlation 155, 156
Simple random sampling 88
Snowball sampling 95
Sorting data 107
Spacing 198
Spearman's rank
   correlation 158, 166
Split-half method 81

Standard deviation 133, 144, 147, 153
Standard error 153
Statistics 152
Stratified sampling 90
Structured interviews 64
Structured questionnaire 70, 80
Summarizing 110
Summary 195
Symmetrical distribution 150
Systematic sampling 91

T

t-test 176
Table of contents 192
Test and re-test method 81
Test of significance 176

Test statistic 184
Thurston technique 76
Thurston-type scale 78
Tippet's tables 88
Total percentage 127
Twofold classification 56
Two-way table 126

U

Uncontrolled interview 65
Unguided interview 65
Undirected interview 65

V

Validity 80, 81, 82
Variability measures 133
Variables 111, 112